Better Homes and Gardens®

ALL-TIME FAVORITE Pies

On the cover: Favorite pies from your kitchen— clockwise from back: *Apple Crumble Pie, Lemon Meringue Pie, Raspberry-Cherry Pie, Cranberry-Pecan Pie,* and *Strawberry Chiffon Pie.* (See index for recipe pages.)

BETTER HOMES AND GARDENS® BOOKS
Editor: Gerald Knox
Art Director: Ernest Shelton
Associate Art Director: Randall Yontz
Production and Copy Editors: David Kirchner,
    Paul S. Kitzke
All-Time Favorite Pies Editors:
    Sandra Granseth, Senior Food Editor
    Patricia Teberg, Associate Food Editor
Food Editor: Doris Eby
Senior Associate Food Editor: Sharyl Heiken
Senior Food Editor: Elizabeth Woolever
Associate Food Editors: Diane Nelson,
    Flora Szatkowski
Recipe Development Editor: Marion Viall
All-Time Favorite Pies Designer: Linda Ford
Senior Graphic Designer: Harijs Priekulis
Graphic Designers: Faith Berven, Richard Lewis,
    Sheryl Veenschoten, Neoma Alt West

Our seal assures you that every recipe in
All-Time Favorite Pies is endorsed
by the Better Homes and Gardens Test Kitchen.
Each recipe is tested for family appeal,
practicality, and deliciousness.

Contents

This selection of homemade favorites includes (clockwise from back) *Deep-Dish Peach Pie*, *Mincemeat Alaska Pie*, *Raspberry Chiffon Pie*, *Chocolate-Cherry Cream Torte*, *Quick Cherry Turnover*, and *Peanut-Ice Cream Pie*. (See index for recipe pages.)

FAVORITE HOMEMADE PIES

Pies, pies, and more pies! Here's a tempting array of fruit, cream, refrigerated and chiffon, custard, and ice cream pies—plus tortes, tarts, and turnovers. Most of the pies make eight servings except the very rich ones, and they'll serve ten. And to help you learn the basics of pie making, we illustrate assembling each type of pie, and include tips for making perfect pie crusts and meringues.

1 Fabulous Fruit Pies

Bake a juicy fruit pie to satisfy your dessert appetite. This chapter is brimming with fresh-tasting pie recipes, as well as tips on how to make them like an expert.

Cherry Pie
(see recipe, opposite)

Create a Fruit Pie

Cherry Pie

2 **16-ounce cans pitted tart red cherries (water pack)**

1½ **cups sugar**

⅓ **cup cornstarch**

Dash salt

1 **tablespoon butter *or* margarine**

3 **or 4 drops almond extract**

10 **drops red food coloring (optional)**

Pastry for Double-Crust Pie (see recipe, page 87)

Milk *and* sugar (optional)

1 Drain cherries; reserve 1 cup liquid. **2** In a medium saucepan combine ¾ *cup* of the sugar, the cornstarch, and salt; stir in reserved cherry liquid. **3** Cook and stir over medium heat till thickened and bubbly. Cook and stir 1 minute more. **4** Remove from heat. Stir in remaining ¾ cup sugar, the cherries, butter or margarine, and almond extract. If desired, stir in food coloring. Let stand while preparing pastry.

5 Prepare and roll out pastry. Line a 9-inch pie plate with *half* of the pastry. Trim to ½ inch beyond edge of pie plate. Turn cherry filling into pastry-lined pie plate. **6** Cut remaining pastry into ½-inch-wide strips. Weave strips atop filling to make lattice crust; flute edge. Brush top of pastry with some milk and sprinkle with sugar, if desired. To prevent overbrowning, cover edge of pie with foil. Bake in 375° oven for 25 minutes. Remove foil; bake for 25 to 30 minutes more or till crust is golden. Cool pie on rack before serving.

1

Drain the cherries by pouring them into a sieve over a large measuring cup or a bowl. Allow the cherry liquid to drain into the cup or bowl.

Reserve 1 cup of the cherry liquid; discard remaining liquid or reserve it for another use. Set well-drained cherries aside.

2

In a medium saucepan stir together ¾ cup of the sugar, the cornstarch, and salt. Blend the cornstarch thoroughly with the sugar so that the starch particles are separated by sugar to prevent lumps from forming.

Slowly stir in the reserved cherry liquid till the mixture is smooth.

3

Cook and stir over medium heat till the mixture is thickened and bubbly. Mixture will bubble over entire surface. Cook and stir 1 minute more so cornstarch will be thoroughly cooked and filling will not taste starchy.

Stir constantly to prevent sticking and scorching.

4 Remove saucepan from heat. Stir in the remaining ¾ cup sugar, the drained cherries, butter or margarine, and almond extract. If desired, stir in about 10 drops of red food coloring. Set the hot cherry filling aside while preparing the pastry.

5 Prepare and roll out the pastry as directed in the recipe on page 87. Line a 9-inch pie plate with *half* of the pastry. Trim pastry to ½ inch beyond the edge of the pie plate.

Pour the cooked cherry filling into the prepared pastry, as shown.

6 Adjust lattice crust, referring to steps 1-5 on page 89. Brush pastry with some milk and sprinkle with a little sugar, if desired. To prevent over-browning, cover edge of pie with foil.

Bake in 375° oven for 25 minutes. Remove foil; bake for 25 to 30 minutes more or till crust is golden.

All-American Apple Pie   (pictured on page 12)

Pastry for Double-Crust Pie (see recipe, page 87)
6 **cups thinly sliced cooking apples (2 pounds)**
1 **tablespoon lemon juice (optional)**
1 **cup sugar**
2 **tablespoons all-purpose flour**
½ **to 1 teaspoon ground cinnamon**
  Dash ground nutmeg
1 **tablespoon butter *or* margarine**
  Sugar (optional)

Prepare and roll out pastry. Line a 9-inch pie plate with *half* of the pastry. Trim pastry to edge of pie plate.

1 If apples lack tartness, sprinkle with the 1 tablespoon lemon juice. **2** In mixing bowl combine sugar, flour, cinnamon, and nutmeg. (For a very juicy pie, omit the flour.) **3** Add sugar mixture to the sliced apples; toss to mix. **4** Fill pastry-lined pie plate with apple mixture; dot with butter or margarine. Cut slits in top crust for escape of steam; place pastry atop filling. Seal and flute edge. **5** Sprinkle some sugar atop, if desired. To prevent overbrowning, cover edge of pie with foil. Bake in 375° oven for 25 minutes. Remove foil; bake for 20 to 25 minutes more or till crust is golden. Cool pie on rack. Serve with vanilla ice cream, if desired.

1

Place the thin apple slices in a large mixing bowl. Use cooking apples such as winesap, jonathan, or McIntosh. If the apples you choose are not very tart, sprinkle with the 1 tablespoon lemon juice. If the apples are already tart, the lemon juice is not needed.

2

In another bowl stir together the sugar, flour, cinnamon, and nutmeg. Blend the flour thoroughly with the sugar so that the starch granules are separated by sugar.

If you like a spicy apple pie, use the larger amount of cinnamon. For a more delicate hint of spice, use the smaller amount.

For a very juicy pie, omit the all-purpose flour.

3

Add the sugar-flour mixture to the apple slices in the large mixing bowl. Using a wooden spoon, gently toss the apple slices with the sugar-flour mixture. When you are finished, the apples should be thoroughly coated with the mixture.

4

Turn the apple slices into the prepared pastry, mounding slightly in the center. Dot with cut-up butter or margarine.

Cut slits in top crust for escape of steam; place pastry atop filling. Seal and flute edge as directed in steps 3-5 on pages 87 and 88.

5

Sprinkle top crust with sugar, if desired. To prevent overbrowning, cover edge of pie with foil.

Bake in 375° oven for 25 minutes. Remove foil; bake for 20 to 25 minutes more or till crust is golden. Cool pie on rack. Serve with vanilla ice cream, if desired.

Pie-Making Tips

• Glaze the top crust of double-crust pies to make them look and taste special. Brush the unbaked crust with milk, water, or melted butter; then sprinkle lightly with sugar. *Or,* just brush the crust lightly with beaten egg or a light coating of milk before baking the pie.

• Avoid messy spills in the oven: set the pie plate on a baking sheet on the oven rack. The pan catches any juice if the pie bubbles over.

• You can store fruit pies at room temperature for a short period of time. But cover and refrigerate any pies with fillings containing eggs or dairy products.

Apple Crumble Pie (pictured on the cover)

Pastry for Single-Crust Pie
(see recipe, page 84)
1 **cup sugar**
2 **tablespoons all-purpose flour**
1 **teaspoon finely shredded lemon peel**
6 **cups thinly sliced, peeled cooking apples (2 pounds)**
3 **tablespoons lemon juice**
½ **cup all-purpose flour**
½ **teaspoon ground cinnamon**
¼ **teaspoon ground ginger**
⅛ **teaspoon ground mace**
¼ **cup butter *or* margarine**

Prepare and roll out pastry. Line a 9-inch pie plate. Trim pastry to ½ inch beyond edge. Flute edge; do not prick.

In mixing bowl stir together ½ *cup* of the sugar, the 2 tablespoons flour, and the lemon peel; set aside. Sprinkle apple slices with lemon juice. Toss apples with sugar mixture to coat. Turn apples into pastry-lined pie plate.

Combine the remaining ½ cup sugar, the ½ cup flour, cinnamon, ginger, and mace. Cut in the butter or margarine till crumbly; sprinkle atop the apple slices.

To prevent overbrowning, cover edge of pie with foil. Bake in 375° oven for 30 minutes. Remove foil; bake for 30 minutes more or till topping is golden. Serve pie warm with vanilla ice cream, or cheddar or American cheese slices, if desired.

Sour Cream-Apple Pie

Pastry for Single-Crust Pie
(see recipe, page 84)
2 **slightly beaten eggs**
1 **cup dairy sour cream**
1 **cup granulated sugar**
2 **tablespoons all-purpose flour**
1 **teaspoon vanilla**
¼ **teaspoon salt**
3 **cups coarsely chopped, peeled cooking apples (about 1 pound)**
3 **tablespoons butter *or* margarine**
¼ **cup packed brown sugar**
¼ **cup all-purpose flour**

Prepare and roll out pastry. Line a 9-inch pie plate. Trim pastry to ½ inch beyond edge of pie plate. Flute edge; do not prick pastry.

In mixing bowl combine eggs and sour cream; stir in granulated sugar, the 2 tablespoons flour, the vanilla, and salt. Stir in apples. Pour apple mixture into pastry-lined pie plate. To prevent overbrowning, cover edge of pie with foil. Bake in 375° oven for 15 minutes.

Meanwhile, melt butter; stir in brown sugar and the ¼ cup flour. Remove foil from pie. Dot top of pie with brown sugar mixture. Bake for 20 to 25 minutes more or till filling is set. Cool thoroughly on rack. Cover; chill to store.

Apple Dumplings

2¼ **cups all-purpose flour**
½ **teaspoon salt**
⅔ **cup shortening**
6 **to 8 tablespoons cold water**
6 **small cooking apples, peeled and cored**
⅔ **cup sugar**
¼ **cup light cream**
⅛ **teaspoon ground nutmeg**
¾ **cup maple-flavored syrup**
Light cream

Mix flour and salt. Cut in shortening till pieces are the size of small peas. Sprinkle *1 tablespoon* water over part of the mixture; gently toss with fork. Push to side of bowl; repeat till all is moistened. Form dough into a ball. On a lightly floured surface, roll out to an 18x12-inch rectangle; cut into six 6-inch squares.

Place an apple in center of *each* square. Mix sugar, the ¼ cup light cream, and nutmeg; spoon about *1½ tablespoons* into center of each apple. Moisten edges of each pastry square with a little water. Fold corners of each square to center; seal by pinching together. Place in an ungreased 11x7x1½-inch baking pan. Bake in 375° oven for 35 minutes. Pour maple-flavored syrup over dumplings. Return to oven and bake 15 minutes more or till apples are done. Serve the dumplings warm with additional light cream. Makes 6.

Deep-Dish Apple Pie

Pastry for Single-Crust Pie
(see recipe, page 84)
1 cup sugar
⅓ cup all-purpose flour*
1 teaspoon ground cinnamon
½ teaspoon ground allspice
¼ teaspoon salt
12 cups thinly sliced, peeled
cooking apples (4 pounds)
3 tablespoons butter *or* margarine
Milk *and* sugar
Light cream *or* cheddar cheese

Prepare pastry. Roll out to a 13x8½-inch rectangle; cut slits in pastry. Combine sugar, flour, cinnamon, allspice, and salt; mix lightly with apples. Turn into a 12x7½x2-inch baking dish (apples will mound higher than sides). Dot with butter or margarine. Carefully place pastry atop apples; flute to the sides but not over the edge. Brush with milk and sprinkle with sugar. To prevent overbrowning, cover edge of pie with foil. Bake in 375° oven for 25 minutes. Remove foil; bake for 20 to 25 minutes more or till crust is golden. Serve warm in dishes; pass light cream or cheddar cheese.

Note: If you like a very juicy pie, use ¼ cup flour.

Apple-Chocolate Chip Pie

Pastry for Single-Crust Pie
(see recipe, page 84)
⅓ cup sugar
1 teaspoon ground cinnamon
1 20-ounce can pie-sliced apples,
drained
⅓ cup semisweet chocolate pieces
1 cup packaged biscuit mix
¼ cup sugar
¼ cup butter *or* margarine

Prepare and roll out pastry. Line a 9-inch pie plate. Trim pastry to ½ inch beyond edge. Flute edge; do not prick.

In mixing bowl combine the ⅓ cup sugar and cinnamon; stir in apples. Turn apple mixture into pastry-lined pie plate. Sprinkle chocolate pieces atop apples. In small bowl combine biscuit mix and the ¼ cup sugar. Cut in butter or margarine till pieces are the size of small peas. Sprinkle mixture over pie. To prevent overbrowning, cover edge of pie with foil. Bake in 375° oven for 25 minutes. Remove foil; bake for 20 to 25 minutes more. Cool thoroughly on rack before serving.

Apple Turnovers

3 cups all-purpose flour
1 teaspoon salt
1 cup shortening
6 to 8 tablespoons cold water
6 tablespoons butter *or*
margarine, softened
1½ pounds cooking apples
1 tablespoon lemon juice
⅔ cup sugar
½ teaspoon ground cinnamon
¼ teaspoon ground nutmeg
⅛ teaspoon salt
Milk, sugar, *and* ground
cinnamon
Vanilla ice cream (optional)

Mix flour and the 1 teaspoon salt. Cut in shortening till pieces are the size of small peas. Sprinkle *1 tablespoon* water over part of the mixture; gently toss with fork. Push to side of bowl; repeat till all is moistened. Form dough into a ball. Divide dough in half. On lightly floured surface, roll *each half* to an 11-inch square. Spread each square with *3 tablespoons* butter or margarine. Fold each square into thirds; chill 30 minutes. Roll each chilled pastry portion to an 18x12-inch rectangle. Cut each rectangle into six 6-inch squares.

Meanwhile, peel and core apples; chop apples. Sprinkle apples with lemon juice. Combine the ⅔ cup sugar, the ½ teaspoon cinnamon, nutmeg, and the ⅛ teaspoon salt; toss with apples. Put about ⅓ *cup* of the apple mixture just off-center on a pastry square. Moisten edges of pastry with a little water. Fold in half diagonally; seal by pressing with tines of fork. Place turnover on ungreased baking sheet. Prick top. Brush with milk; sprinkle with additional sugar and cinnamon. Repeat with the remaining pastry squares. Bake in 375° oven for 30 to 35 minutes or till crust is golden. Serve with ice cream, if desired. Makes 12.

A juicy wedge of freshly baked *All-American Apple Pie* (see recipe, page 8) will turn any day into a special occasion. Serve a scoop of vanilla ice cream atop each slice.

Apple-Banana Crunch Pie

¼ **cup butter** *or* **margarine**
Pastry for Single-Crust Pie
(see recipe, page 84)
1 **20-ounce can pie-sliced apples,**
drained
2 **medium bananas, peeled and**
cut into chunks (2 cups)
2 **tablespoons lemon juice**
½ **cup all-purpose flour**
¼ **cup granulated sugar**
¼ **cup packed brown sugar**
¼ **teaspoon ground cinnamon**
¼ **teaspoon ground nutmeg**

Bring butter to room temperature. Meanwhile, prepare and roll out pastry. Line a 9-inch pie plate. Trim pastry to ½ inch beyond edge of pie plate. Flute edge; do not prick. Bake in 375° oven for 5 to 7 minutes or till lightly browned. Cool.

In bowl combine drained apples, bananas, and lemon juice; let stand 10 minutes. Meanwhile, to make crumb mixture, combine flour, granulated sugar, brown sugar, cinnamon, and nutmeg; cut in softened butter till crumbly. Place apples and bananas in the baked pastry shell. Sprinkle crumb mixture atop fruit. To prevent overbrowning, cover edge of pie with foil. Bake in 375° oven for 20 minutes. Remove foil; bake for 20 minutes more. Cool on rack before serving.

Hawaiian Apple Pie (pictured on page 83)

Pastry for Single-Crust Pie
(see recipe, page 84)
1 12-ounce can (1½ cups)
   unsweetened pineapple juice
¾ cup sugar
7 cooking apples, peeled, cored,
   and cut into wedges
   (about 2¼ pounds)
3 tablespoons cornstarch
1 tablespoon butter or margarine
½ teaspoon salt
½ teaspoon vanilla
   Unsweetened whipped cream
   Chopped macadamia nuts or
   peanuts

Prepare and roll out pastry. Line a 9-inch pie plate. Trim pastry to ½ inch beyond edge of pie plate. Flute edge; prick pastry. Bake in 450° oven for 10 to 12 minutes or till pastry is golden. Cool on rack.

For the pie filling, in large saucepan combine 1¼ cups of the pineapple juice and sugar. Bring to boiling; add apples. Simmer, covered, 3 to 4 minutes or till apples are tender but not soft. With slotted spoon, lift apples from pineapple liquid; set aside to drain. Slowly blend remaining pineapple juice into cornstarch; add to hot pineapple mixture in saucepan. Cook and stir till thickened and bubbly; cook 1 minute more. Remove from heat; stir in butter or margarine, salt, and vanilla. Cool 30 minutes without stirring. Pour half of the filling into the baked pastry shell; spread to cover bottom. Arrange apple wedges atop. Spoon remaining filling over apples. Cover; chill. Garnish pie with whipped cream and chopped macadamia nuts or peanuts.

Apricot Pie

Pastry for Double-Crust Pie
(see recipe, page 87)
4 cups sliced, pitted fresh or
   frozen apricots (2 pounds
   fresh)
1 tablespoon lemon juice
1 cup sugar
¼ cup all-purpose flour
⅛ teaspoon ground nutmeg
1 tablespoon butter or margarine

Prepare and roll out pastry. Line a 9-inch pie plate with half of the pastry. Trim pastry to edge of plate.

In large bowl sprinkle the apricots with lemon juice. Combine the sugar, flour, and ground nutmeg; toss with the sliced apricots. Turn apricot mixture into pastry-lined pie plate; dot with butter or margarine. Cut slits in top crust; place pastry atop filling. Seal and flute edge. To prevent overbrowning, cover edge of pie with foil. Bake in 375° oven for 20 minutes. Remove foil; bake for 20 to 25 minutes more or till crust is golden. Cool thoroughly on rack before serving.

Apricot-Pineapple Pie

Pastry for Double-Crust Pie
(see recipe, page 87)
1 8-ounce package (2 cups) dried
   apricots
   Water
¾ cup sugar
2 tablespoons all-purpose flour
1 20-ounce can crushed
   pineapple
1 tablespoon butter or margarine

Prepare and roll out pastry. Line a 9-inch pie plate with half of the pastry. Trim pastry to edge of plate.

Halve apricots. In large saucepan, cover apricots with water; bring to boiling. Simmer gently, covered, for 15 to 20 minutes or till tender. Drain. In mixing bowl combine sugar and flour; add drained apricots and undrained pineapple. Toss to mix thoroughly. Turn fruit mixture into pastry-lined pie plate; dot with butter.

Cut slits in top crust; place pastry atop filling. Seal and flute edge. To prevent overbrowning, cover edge of pie with foil. Bake in 375° oven for 25 minutes. Remove foil; bake for 20 to 25 minutes more. Cool thoroughly on rack before serving.

Cherry-Cheese Pizza Pie

1¾ cups all-purpose flour
½ cup butter *or* margarine
3 tablespoons shortening
1 beaten egg yolk
3 tablespoons ice water
1 8-ounce package cream cheese, softened
½ cup sugar
2 eggs
⅓ cup chopped walnuts
1 teaspoon vanilla
⅔ cup sugar
2 tablespoons cornstarch
½ cup water
3 cups fresh *or* frozen pitted tart red cherries (16 ounces)
1 tablespoon butter *or* margarine
Few drops almond extract
Few drops red food coloring
Unsweetened whipped cream

Combine flour and ¾ teaspoon *salt;* cut in the ½ cup butter or margarine and shortening till pieces are the size of fine crumbs. Combine egg yolk and the 3 tablespoons ice water; gradually add to flour mixture and mix well. Using fingers, knead lightly to form a ball. Cover; chill pastry for ½ to 1 hour. Roll pastry to a 13-inch circle. Line a 12-inch pizza pan with pastry. Trim pastry to ½ inch beyond edge of pan. Flute edge; prick pastry. Bake in 350° oven for 15 minutes. Meanwhile, reroll trimmings to ⅛-inch thickness. Cut into desired shapes with small cookie cutter. Place cutouts on ungreased baking sheet. Bake in 350° oven for 6 to 8 minutes. Cool.

In mixer bowl combine cream cheese and ½ cup sugar; beat with electric mixer till fluffy. Beat in eggs. Stir in nuts and vanilla. Pour cheese mixture into crust. Bake in 350° oven for 12 to 15 minutes more or till set. Cool.

In saucepan stir together the ⅔ cup sugar, the cornstarch, and dash *salt*. Add the ½ cup water; cook and stir over medium heat till thickened and bubbly. Remove from heat. Stir in cherries, the 1 tablespoon butter, almond extract, and food coloring. Spread cherry mixture over cheese layer. Chill. To serve, garnish with whipped cream and pastry cutouts.

Cherry-Almond Tarts

Pastry for Single-Crust Pie (see recipe, page 84)
1 16-ounce can pitted tart red cherries (water-pack)
Water
½ cup sugar
2 tablespoons cornstarch
Several drops almond extract
Unsweetened whipped cream
2 tablespoons chopped toasted almonds

Prepare pastry. Roll out to ⅛-inch thickness. Cut pastry into six 4½-inch circles. Fit dough circles over inverted muffin cups, pinching pleats at intervals to fit around the cups; prick. Place muffin cups on baking sheet. Bake in 450° oven for 7 to 10 minutes or till golden. Cool.

Drain cherries, reserving liquid; set aside. Add enough water to cherry liquid to measure 1 cup liquid. In saucepan stir together sugar and cornstarch; slowly stir in cherry liquid. Add cherries. Cook and stir over medium heat till thickened and bubbly. Stir in almond extract. Spoon mixture into baked tart shells. Chill. Top with whipped cream; sprinkle with toasted almonds. Makes 6.

Cherry-Brandy Pie

Pastry for Double-Crust Pie (see recipe, page 87)
4 cups fresh *or* frozen pitted tart red cherries (20 ounces)
1 cup sugar
3 tablespoons quick-cooking tapioca
1 tablespoon cherry brandy
1 teaspoon finely shredded lemon peel
Butter *or* margarine

Prepare and roll out pastry. Line a 9-inch pie plate with *half* of the pastry. Trim pastry to edge of pie plate.

In large bowl combine cherries, sugar, tapioca, brandy, lemon peel, and ⅛ teaspoon *salt.* Let stand 20 minutes, stirring occasionally. Turn mixture into pastry-lined pie plate. Dot with butter or margarine. Cut slits in top crust; place pastry atop filling. Seal and flute edge high. To prevent overbrowning, cover edge of pie with foil. Bake in 375° oven for 30 minutes. Remove foil; bake for 25 to 30 minutes more or till golden. Cool pie on rack before serving.

Quick Cherry Turnover (pictured on page 4)

Pastry for Double-Crust Pie
  (see recipe, page 87)
1 21-ounce can cherry pie filling*
¼ cup chopped toasted almonds
½ cup sifted powdered sugar
1 tablespoon butter *or* margarine,
  softened
¼ teaspoon vanilla
  Milk

Prepare pastry. Roll out *half* of the pastry to make an even 11-inch circle. Place pastry circle on a baking sheet.

In mixing bowl combine pie filling and almonds; spoon *half* over center of half of pastry circle, leaving a 1½-inch edge along the outside. Gently lift and fold other half of pastry over filling. Seal edge; turn up ½ inch of edge and flute. Cut small slits in top. Repeat with remaining pastry and pie filling mixture. Bake in 425° oven for 30 minutes or till golden.

Meanwhile, to prepare glaze, in mixing bowl stir together powdered sugar, butter or margarine, and vanilla. Stir in enough milk to make of drizzling consistency. Drizzle glaze over warm turnover. Makes 2.

Note: Or, substitute blueberry, strawberry, or apple pie filling.

Peach-Orange Pie

Pastry for Double-Crust Pie
  (see recipe, page 87)
¾ cup sugar
1 teaspoon finely shredded
  orange peel
2 tablespoons all-purpose flour
4 cups sliced fresh peaches
  (2 pounds)
2 large oranges, peeled and
  sectioned (about ⅔ cup)*
2 tablespoons butter *or* margarine

Prepare and roll out pastry. Line a 9-inch pie plate with *half* of the pastry. Trim to ½ inch beyond edge of pie plate.

In mixing bowl stir together sugar, orange peel, and flour; blend in peaches and oranges. Turn into pastry-lined pie plate. Dot with butter. Cut remaining pastry into ½-inch-wide strips. Weave strips atop filling to make lattice crust; flute edge. To prevent overbrowning, cover edge of pie with foil. Bake in 375° oven for 30 minutes. Remove foil; bake for 30 to 40 minutes more. Cool.

Note: To section an orange, first cut off the peel and white membrane. Remove sections by cutting into center of orange between fruit and the membrane of each section. Then turn the knife and slide it down the other side of the section next to the membrane. Remove any seeds.

Peach-Cranberry Pie

1 29-ounce can peach slices
3 cups fresh cranberries
1½ cups sugar
3 tablespoons cornstarch
¼ cup chopped toasted almonds
  Pastry for Double-Crust Pie
  (see recipe, page 87)

Drain peaches, reserving 1 cup syrup; coarsely cut up peaches and set aside. In saucepan combine cranberries and reserved peach syrup; cook 5 to 8 minutes or till skins of cranberries pop. Combine sugar and cornstarch. Stir into hot cranberries. Cook quickly, stirring constantly, till mixture is thickened and bubbly. Remove from heat. Stir in peaches and almonds; set aside to cool.

Prepare and roll out pastry. Line a 9-inch pie plate with *half* of the pastry. Trim pastry to ½ inch beyond edge of pie plate. Pour peach mixture into pastry-lined pie plate. Cut remaining pastry into ½-inch-wide strips. Weave strips atop filling to make lattice crust; flute edge. To prevent overbrowning, cover edge of pie with foil. Bake in 375° oven for 20 minutes. Remove foil; bake for 20 to 25 minutes more. Cool on rack before serving.

French Crunch Peach Pie delights dessert lovers with its scrumptious peach filling.
And, the buttery crumb and toasted almond topping makes it a delicious peach pie variation.

French Crunch Peach Pie

Pastry for Single-Crust Pie
(see recipe, page 84)
2 eggs
1 tablespoon lemon juice
⅓ cup sugar
1 29-ounce can *and* 1 16-ounce
can peach slices, drained
1 cup finely crushed vanilla
wafers (22 wafers)
½ cup chopped toasted almonds
¼ cup butter *or* margarine, melted
Vanilla ice cream *or* cheddar
cheese triangles

Prepare and roll out pastry. Line a 9-inch pie plate. Trim pastry to ½ inch beyond edge of pie plate. Flute edge; do not prick pastry. Bake in 450° oven for 5 minutes.

In mixing bowl beat eggs and lemon juice till blended; stir in sugar. Fold in drained peaches. Turn peach mixture into the partially baked pastry shell. Stir together vanilla wafer crumbs, almonds, and butter or margarine; sprinkle over peach mixture. To prevent overbrowning, cover edge of pie with foil. Bake in 375° oven for 20 minutes. Remove foil; bake for 20 to 25 minutes more or till filling is set in center. Cool on rack before serving. Cover; chill to store. Serve with scoops of ice cream or cheese triangles.

Deep-Dish Peach Pie (pictured on page 4)

¾ cup sugar
3 tablespoons all-purpose flour
¼ teaspoon ground nutmeg
6 cups peeled, thickly sliced fresh
peaches (3 pounds)
3 tablespoons grenadine syrup
2 tablespoons lemon juice
2 tablespoons butter *or* margarine
Pastry for Single-Crust Pie
(see recipe, page 84)

In large bowl combine sugar, flour, and nutmeg; add peaches and toss till well-coated. Let mixture stand 5 minutes. Carefully stir in grenadine and lemon juice. Turn mixture into a 1½-quart casserole or a 10-inch round deep baking dish, spreading peaches evenly; dot with butter or margarine.

Prepare and roll out pastry to an even 9-inch or 11-inch circle (depending on dish size). Cut slits in pastry. Place over peach mixture in baking dish. Trim pastry; flute to sides of dish but not over edge. To prevent overbrowning, cover edge with foil. Place dish on baking sheet in oven. Bake in 375° oven for 25 minutes. Remove foil; bake for 30 to 35 minutes more or till crust is golden. Cool on rack before serving.

Golden Peach Pie

Pastry for Double-Crust Pie
(see recipe, page 86)
1 29-ounce can *and* 1 16-ounce
can peach slices
½ cup sugar
2 tablespoons all-purpose flour
½ teaspoon ground nutmeg
Dash salt
3 tablespoons butter *or* margarine
½ teaspoon finely shredded
lemon peel
4 teaspoons lemon juice
Several drops almond extract
Milk *and* sugar

Prepare and roll out pastry. Line a 9-inch pie plate with *half* of the pastry. Trim pastry to edge of plate.

Drain peaches, reserving ⅓ cup syrup; cut up large peach slices. In saucepan stir together sugar, flour, nutmeg, and salt; add reserved syrup. Cook and stir till mixture is thickened and bubbly. Remove from heat. Stir in butter or margarine, lemon peel, lemon juice, and almond extract; add drained peaches.

Turn mixture into pastry-lined pie plate. Cut slits in top crust; place pastry atop filling. Seal and flute edge. Brush with a little milk and sprinkle with some sugar. To prevent overbrowning, cover edge of pie with foil. Bake in 375° oven for 20 minutes. Remove foil and bake 25 to 30 minutes more or till crust is golden. Serve pie warm.

Homemade Mincemeat Pie

1 **pound beef stew meat**
4 **pounds cooking apples, peeled,**
   cored, and quartered
   (9 cups)
4 **ounces suet**
2½ **cups sugar**
2½ **cups water**
1 **15-ounce package raisins**
2 **cups dried currants**
   (9 ounces)
½ **cup diced mixed candied fruits**
   and peels
1 **teaspoon finely shredded**
   orange peel
1 **cup orange juice**
1 **teaspoon finely shredded lemon**
   peel
¼ **cup lemon juice**
1 **teaspoon salt**
½ **teaspoon ground nutmeg**
¼ **teaspoon ground mace**
   Pastry for Double-Crust Pie*
   (see recipe, page 87)
   Milk
   Brandy Hard Sauce

In large saucepan combine beef stew meat and enough water to cover. Cover and simmer for 2 hours or till tender. Drain; cool. Using coarse blade of food grinder, grind cooked beef, apples, and suet. In large kettle combine sugar, the 2½ cups water, raisins, currants, mixed candied fruits and peels, orange peel, orange juice, lemon peel, lemon juice, salt, nutmeg, and mace; stir in ground meat-apple mixture. Cover and simmer 45 minutes; stir mixture frequently.

Prepare and roll out pastry. Line a 9-inch pie plate with *half* of the pastry. Trim pastry to edge of pie plate. Fill pastry-lined pie plate with *4 cups* of the meat mixture. (Freeze remaining mincemeat in 4-cup portions.)* Cut slits in top crust (or cut a design in pastry with a small cookie cutter). Place pastry atop filling. Seal and flute edge. Brush with a little milk. To prevent overbrowning, cover edge of pie with foil. Bake in 375° oven for 20 minutes. Remove foil; bake about 15 minutes more or till crust is golden. Cool on rack before serving. Serve with Brandy Hard Sauce. Cover; chill to store.

Brandy Hard Sauce: Thoroughly cream together 2 cups sifted *powdered sugar,* ½ cup softened *butter or margarine,* and 1 teaspoon *brandy.* Stir in 1 beaten *egg yolk;* fold in 1 stiff-beaten *egg white.* Chill.

*Note: This recipe makes enough mincemeat for 3 pies.

Mince-Apple Pie

Pastry for Double-Crust Pie
(see recipe, page 87)
3 **cups thinly sliced, peeled**
   cooking apples
   (about 1 pound)
1 **28-ounce jar (2⅔ cups)**
   prepared mincemeat
2 **tablespoons lemon juice**
   Milk *and* sugar
   Brandy Hard Sauce
   (see recipe above)

Prepare and roll out pastry. Line a 9-inch pie plate with *half* of the pastry. Trim pastry to edge of pie plate.

In mixing bowl combine sliced apples, mincemeat, and lemon juice. Pour mixture into pastry-lined pie plate. Cut slits in top crust; place pastry atop filling. Seal and flute edge. Brush with some milk and sprinkle with a little sugar. To prevent overbrowning, cover edge of pie with foil. Bake in 375° oven for 25 minutes. Remove foil; bake about 25 minutes more or till crust is golden. Cool on rack before serving. Serve with Brandy Hard Sauce.

Mince-Peach Pie

Pastry for Double-Crust Pie
(see recipe, page 87)
1 **28-ounce jar (2⅔ cups)**
   prepared mincemeat
1 **29-ounce can peach slices,**
   drained
   Milk *and* sugar

Prepare and roll out pastry. Line a 9-inch pie plate with *half* of the pastry. Trim pastry to edge of pie plate.

In mixing bowl combine prepared mincemeat and drained peaches. Pour mixture into pastry-lined pie plate. Cut slits in top crust; place pastry atop filling. Seal and flute edge. Brush top with a little milk and sprinkle with some sugar. To prevent overbrowning, cover edge of pie with foil. Bake in 375° oven for 25 minutes. Remove foil; bake about 25 minutes more or till crust is golden. Cool on rack before serving.

For holiday entertaining, create a sensation with *Homemade Mincemeat Pie.* And add to the rich, delicious flavor by serving a dollop of fluffy *Brandy Hard Sauce* atop each piece.

Banana-Nut Turnovers

Pastry for Double-Crust Pie
(see recipe, page 87)
4 **medium bananas**
2 **tablespoons lemon juice**
½ **cup chopped pecans**
⅓ **cup packed brown sugar**
¾ **teaspoon ground cinnamon**
Milk *and* granulated sugar

Prepare pastry; divide in half. On floured surface, roll and trim *each half* to a 12-inch square. Cut each half into four 6-inch squares. Peel bananas; slice *half* a banana onto *each* pastry square. Sprinkle *each* with a little lemon juice. Top *each* with 1 tablespoon chopped pecans. Combine brown sugar and cinnamon; sprinkle about 1 tablespoon over each square. Fold each pastry square in half diagonally; moisten edges and seal. Place on ungreased baking sheet. Brush with milk; sprinkle with granulated sugar. Bake in 375° oven for 25 to 30 minutes or till golden. Cool. Makes 8.

Fruit Cup Pie

Pastry for Double-Crust Pie
(see recipe, page 87)
¾ **cup sugar**
¼ **cup quick-cooking tapioca**
¼ **teaspoon ground cinnamon**
¼ **teaspoon ground nutmeg**
2 **cups diced fresh peaches**
2 **cups diced fresh pears**
1 **cup seedless green grapes**
2 **tablespoons chopped**
   maraschino cherries
1 **tablespoon lemon juice**

Prepare and roll out pastry. Line a 9-inch pie plate with *half* of the pastry; trim pastry to edge of pie plate.

In mixing bowl combine sugar, tapioca, cinnamon, nutmeg, and dash *salt*. Add peaches, pears, grapes, maraschino cherries, and lemon juice; toss. Let stand 5 minutes. Turn fruit mixture into the pastry-lined pie plate. Cut slits in top crust for escape of steam; place atop filling. Seal and flute edge. If desired, brush with milk; sprinkle with sugar. To prevent overbrowning, cover edge of pie with foil. Bake in 375° oven for 25 minutes. Remove foil; bake for 20 to 25 minutes longer or till golden. Cool pie on rack before serving.

Gooseberry Pie

Pastry for Double-Crust Pie
(see recipe, page 87)
4 **cups fresh gooseberries *or* 2**
   16-ounce cans gooseberries*
⅔ **to 1 cup sugar**
¼ **cup all-purpose flour***
   Dash salt
1 **tablespoon butter *or* margarine**

Prepare and roll out pastry. Line a 9-inch pie plate with *half* of the pastry; trim pastry to edge of pie plate. Stem and wash fresh gooseberries *or* drain canned berries. Combine sugar, flour, and salt. Stir in berries. Turn into pastry-lined pie plate. Dot with butter. Cut slits in top crust; place atop filling. Seal and flute edge. To prevent overbrowning, cover edge of pie with foil. Bake in 375° oven for 20 minutes. Remove foil; bake for 25 minutes longer or till golden. Cool.

Note: Reduce flour to 3 tablespoons for canned berries.

Fresh Blackberry Pie

Pastry for Double-Crust Pie
(see recipe, page 87)
1¼ **cups sugar**
¼ **cup all-purpose flour**
⅛ **teaspoon salt**
4 **cups fresh blackberries**
   Vanilla ice cream (optional)

Prepare and roll out pastry. Line a 9-inch pie plate with *half* of the pastry; trim pastry to edge of pie plate.

Combine sugar, flour, and salt. Add blackberries, tossing to coat. Pour berry mixture into pastry-lined pie plate. Cut slits in top crust; place atop filling. Seal and flute edge. To prevent overbrowning, cover edge of pie with foil. Bake in 375° oven for 20 minutes. Remove foil; bake for 25 to 30 minutes longer or till golden. Cool on rack. Serve with ice cream, if desired.

Fresh Blueberry Pie

Pastry for Double-Crust Pie
(see recipe, page 87)
5 cups fresh blueberries *or* 1
20-ounce package frozen
unsweetened blueberries,
thawed*
1 cup sugar
¼ cup all-purpose flour*
½ teaspoon finely shredded lemon
peel
2 teaspoons lemon juice
1 tablespoon butter

Prepare and roll out pastry. Line a 9-inch pie plate with *half* of the pastry; trim pastry to edge of pie plate. In mixing bowl combine blueberries, sugar, flour, lemon peel, and dash *salt*. Turn blueberry mixture into pastry-lined pie plate. Drizzle with lemon juice and dot with butter. Cut slits in top crust; place atop filling. Seal and flute edge. To prevent overbrowning, cover edge of pie with foil. Bake in 375° oven for 20 minutes. Remove foil and bake for 20 to 25 minutes longer or till crust is golden. Cool pie on rack before serving.

Note: If using frozen blueberries, increase the all-purpose flour to ⅓ cup.

Glazed Blueberry Pie

Pastry for Single-Crust Pie
(see recipe, page 84)
1 3-ounce package cream cheese,
softened
4 cups fresh blueberries*
½ cup water
¾ cup sugar
3 tablespoons cornstarch
2 tablespoons lemon juice
Unsweetened whipped cream

Prepare and roll out pastry. Line a 9-inch pie plate. Trim pastry ½ inch beyond edge of pie plate. Flute edge; prick pastry. Bake in 450° oven for 10 to 12 minutes or till golden. Cool. Meanwhile, cut daisy-shapes from pastry trimmings. Bake cutouts on baking sheet in 450° oven about 3 minutes or till golden. Set aside to cool. Spread cream cheese in bottom of cooled pastry shell. Chill. Spread *3 cups* of the blueberries atop cream cheese.

In saucepan combine remaining 1 cup blueberries and the water; bring just to boiling. Reduce heat; simmer berries 2 minutes. Sieve cooked mixture (it should yield ½ to ⅔ cup). Combine sugar and cornstarch; gradually stir in sieved blueberry mixture. Cook, stirring constantly, till thickened and bubbly. Cool slightly; stir in lemon juice. Pour over blueberries in pie shell. Cover; chill. Arrange cutouts atop. Garnish with whipped cream.

Note: Do not substitute frozen blueberries for the fresh berries in this recipe; they would make the glaze too thin.

Blueberry Strata Pie

Pastry for Single-Crust Pie
(see recipe, page 84)
1 15-ounce can blueberries
1 8¼-ounce can crushed
pineapple
1 8-ounce package cream cheese,
softened
3 tablespoons sugar
1 tablespoon milk
½ teaspoon vanilla
¼ cup sugar
2 tablespoons cornstarch
¼ teaspoon salt
1 teaspoon lemon juice
½ cup whipping cream

Prepare and roll out pastry. Line a 9-inch pie plate. Trim pastry to ½ inch beyond edge of pie plate. Flute edge; prick pastry. Bake in 450° oven for 10 to 12 minutes or till golden. Cool on rack.

Drain blueberries and pineapple, reserving syrups. Combine softened cream cheese, 3 tablespoons sugar, milk, and vanilla. Reserve 2 tablespoons pineapple; stir remainder into cream cheese mixture. Spread cream cheese mixture over bottom of cooled pastry shell; chill.

In saucepan combine the ¼ cup sugar, cornstarch, and salt. Combine reserved syrups; measure 1¼ cups syrup (discard remaining). Stir syrup into cornstarch mixture. Cook and stir till thickened and bubbly. Stir in blueberries and lemon juice; cool. Pour over chilled cream cheese layer; chill again. Whip cream; spread over pie. Garnish with reserved pineapple. Cover; chill to store.

Spoon into country-style *Deep-Dish Plum Pie.* You'll enjoy the fresh plum flavor sweetened with a hint of brown sugar. It tastes best served warm from the oven with scoops of vanilla ice cream.

Raspberry-Cherry Pie (pictured on the cover)

1 **10-ounce package frozen red raspberries, thawed**
¾ **cup sugar**
3 **tablespoons cornstarch**
¼ **teaspoon salt**
2 **cups fresh *or* frozen tart red cherries**
  Pastry for Double-Crust Pie (see recipe, page 87)

Drain raspberries; reserve syrup. Add enough water to syrup to measure 1 cup liquid. In saucepan mix together sugar, cornstarch, and salt. Stir in reserved raspberry liquid. Stir fresh or frozen cherries into mixture in saucepan. Cook and stir over medium-high heat till thickened and bubbly. Cook and stir mixture 1 minute more. Remove from heat; stir in drained raspberries. Cool 15 to 20 minutes.

Prepare and roll out pastry. Line a 9-inch pie plate with *half* of the pastry; trim pastry ½ inch beyond edge of pie plate. Fill with partially cooled raspberry-cherry mixture. Cut remaining pastry into ½-inch-wide strips. Weave strips atop filling to make lattice crust; flute edges high. To prevent overbrowning, cover edge of pie with foil. Bake in 375° oven for 20 minutes. Remove foil and bake for 15 to 20 minutes more. Cool on rack.

Red Raspberry-Grape Pie

Pastry for Double-Crust Pie
(see recipe, page 87)
1 16-ounce can light seedless
grapes, drained
⅔ cup sugar
⅓ cup all-purpose flour
2 10-ounce packages frozen red
raspberries, thawed
2 tablespoons butter or margarine

Prepare and roll out pastry. Line a 9-inch pie plate with *half* of the pastry; trim pastry ½ inch beyond edge of pie plate. Halve grapes. In mixing bowl stir together sugar and flour; stir in raspberries with syrup and grapes. Fill pastry-lined pie plate with fruit mixture. Dot with butter. Cut slits in top crust for escape of steam; place atop filling. Seal and flute edge. To prevent overbrowning, cover edge of pie with foil. Bake in 375° oven for 25 minutes. Remove foil; bake for 20 to 25 minutes more or till golden. Cool on rack.

Rosy Raspberry Pie

3 tablespoons quick-cooking
tapioca
½ cup sugar
Dash salt
2 10-ounce packages frozen red
raspberries, thawed
Pastry for Double-Crust Pie
(see recipe, page 87)
Vanilla ice cream (optional)

In mixing bowl mix tapioca, sugar, and salt. Gently stir in thawed raspberries with syrup. Let stand 15 minutes.

Prepare and roll out pastry. Line a 9-inch pie plate with *half* of the pastry; trim pastry to edge of pie plate. Fill pastry-lined pie plate with raspberry mixture. Cut slits in top crust; place atop filling. Seal and flute edge. To prevent overbrowning, cover edge of pie with foil. Bake in 375° oven for 25 minutes. Remove foil; bake for 20 to 25 minutes longer or till crust is golden. Cool on rack. Serve with ice cream, if desired.

Fresh Raspberry Pie

Pastry for Double-Crust Pie
(see recipe, page 87)
1 cup sugar
2 tablespoons cornstarch
Dash salt
4 cups fresh or frozen red or
black raspberries
2 tablespoons butter or margarine

Prepare and roll out pastry. Line a 9-inch pie plate with *half* of the pastry. Trim pastry to edge of pie plate. In mixing bowl combine sugar, cornstarch, and salt; Gently stir in berries to coat. Turn berry mixture into pastry-lined pie plate. Dot with butter or margarine. Cut slits in top crust for escape of steam; place atop filling. Seal and flute edge.

To prevent overbrowning, cover edge of pie with foil. Bake in 375° oven for 20 minutes. Remove foil; bake for 20 to 30 minutes longer. Cool on rack.

Deep-Dish Plum Pie

¾ cup packed brown sugar
2 teaspoons quick-cooking
tapioca
¼ teaspoon ground cinnamon
Dash ground nutmeg
5 cups halved pitted fresh purple
plums (2 pounds)
1 tablespoon butter
Pastry for Single-Crust Pie
(see recipe, page 84)
Vanilla ice cream or light cream

In a large mixing bowl combine the brown sugar, tapioca, cinnamon, nutmeg, and dash *salt*. Stir in plums. Let stand 15 minutes. Turn mixture into an 8x1½-inch round baking dish. Dot with butter. Prepare and roll out pastry to a 9-inch circle. Cut slits for escape of steam. Place over plum filling. Trim pastry; flute to side of dish but not over edge. If desired, garnish top of pie with pastry cutouts made from pastry trimmings. To prevent overbrowning, cover edge of pie with foil. Bake in 375° oven for 20 minutes. Remove foil; bake for 20 to 25 minutes longer or till crust is golden. Serve pie warm in dessert dishes; serve with ice cream or light cream.

Raisin Crisscross Pie

1 cup packed brown sugar
2 tablespoons cornstarch
2 cups raisins
1⅓ cups cold water
½ teaspoon finely shredded
 orange peel
½ cup orange juice
½ teaspoon finely shredded lemon
 peel
2 tablespoons lemon juice
½ cup chopped walnuts
 Pastry for Double-Crust Pie
 (see recipe, page 87)
 Vanilla ice cream (optional)

In medium saucepan combine brown sugar and cornstarch. Stir in raisins, water, orange peel, orange juice, lemon peel, and lemon juice. Cook and stir over medium heat till thickened and bubbly; cook and stir 1 minute more. Remove from heat; stir in walnuts.

Prepare and roll out pastry. Line a 9-inch pie plate with *half* of the pastry. Trim pastry to ½ inch beyond edge of pie plate. Pour in raisin mixture. Cut remaining pastry into ½-inch-wide strips. Weave strips atop filling to make lattice crust; flute edge.

To prevent overbrowning, cover edge of pie with foil. Bake in 375° oven for 20 minutes. Remove foil and bake for about 20 minutes more or till crust is golden. Serve warm with vanilla ice cream, if desired.

Fresh Rhubarb Pie

1¼ cups sugar
⅓ cup all-purpose flour
 Dash salt
4 cups rhubarb cut into 1-inch
 pieces
 Pastry for Double-Crust Pie
 (see recipe, page 87)
2 tablespoons butter *or* margarine
 Vanilla ice cream (optional)

In mixing bowl combine sugar, flour, and salt. Stir in rhubarb pieces; toss gently to coat fruit. Let fruit mixture stand for 15 minutes.

Meanwhile, prepare and roll out pastry. Line a 9-inch pie plate with *half* of the pastry. Trim pastry to edge of pie plate. Turn rhubarb mixture into pastry-lined pie plate. Dot with butter or margarine. Cut slits in top crust for escape of steam; place pastry atop filling. Seal and flute edge.

To prevent overbrowning, cover edge of pie with foil. Bake pie in 375° oven for 25 minutes. Remove foil and bake for about 25 minutes more or till golden. Serve warm, or cool on rack before serving. Top each serving with a scoop of vanilla ice cream, if desired.

Rhubarb-Strawberry Pie

1¼ to 1½ cups sugar
3 tablespoons quick-cooking
 tapioca
¼ teaspoon salt
¼ teaspoon ground nutmeg
3 cups rhubarb cut into ½-inch
 pieces (1 pound)
2 cups sliced fresh strawberries
 Pastry for Double-Crust Pie
 (see recipe, page 87)
1 tablespoon butter *or* margarine

In large mixing bowl stir together sugar, quick-cooking tapioca, salt, and ground nutmeg. Add rhubarb pieces and sliced strawberries; toss gently to coat fruit. Let fruit mixture stand for 15 minutes.

Meanwhile, prepare and roll out pastry. Line a 9-inch pie plate with *half* of the pastry. Trim pastry to edge of pie plate. Pour fruit mixture into pastry-lined pie plate. Dot with butter or margarine. Cut slits in top crust for escape of steam; place pastry atop filling. Seal and flute edge.

To prevent overbrowning, cover edge of pie with foil. Bake in 375° oven for 25 minutes. Remove foil; bake for 20 to 25 minutes more or till crust is golden. Cool pie on rack before serving.

Rhubarb-Cherry Pie

3 cups rhubarb cut into ½-inch pieces (1 pound)
1 16-ounce can pitted tart red cherries, drained (water pack)
1¼ cups sugar
3 tablespoons quick-cooking tapioca
Pastry for Double-Crust Pie (see recipe, page 87)

In saucepan combine rhubarb, cherries, sugar, and tapioca; let fruit mixture stand for 15 minutes. Bring fruit mixture to boiling; remove from heat and let cool for 45 minutes.

Prepare and roll out pastry. Line a 9-inch pie plate with *half* of the pastry. Trim pastry to ½ inch beyond edge of pie plate. Pour cooled rhubarb-cherry mixture into pastry-lined pie plate. Cut remaining pastry into ½-inch-wide strips. Weave strips atop filling to make lattice crust; flute edge.

To prevent overbrowning, cover edge of pie with foil. Bake pie in 375° oven for 20 minutes. Remove foil and bake for about 20 minutes more or till crust is golden. Cool pie on rack before serving.

Fresh Pear Crumble Pie

Pastry for Single-Crust Pie (see recipe, page 84)
5 cups peeled, sliced fresh pears (about 2½ pounds)
3 tablespoons lemon juice
½ cup sugar
2 tablespoons all-purpose flour
1 teaspoon finely shredded lemon peel
½ cup all-purpose flour
½ cup sugar
½ teaspoon ground ginger
½ teaspoon ground cinnamon
⅛ teaspoon ground mace
¼ cup butter *or* margarine
3 slices American *or* cheddar cheese, cut into triangles (optional)

Prepare and roll out pastry. Line a 9-inch pie plate. Trim pastry to ½ inch beyond edge of pie plate. Flute edge; do not prick pastry.

In a bowl sprinkle pears with lemon juice. In a large mixing bowl combine ½ cup sugar, the 2 tablespoons flour, and lemon peel; stir in sliced pears. Spoon pear-sugar mixture into pastry-lined plate.

In another mixing bowl combine the ½ cup flour, ½ cup sugar, ginger, cinnamon, and mace. Cut in butter or margarine till mixture resembles coarse crumbs. Sprinkle crumb mixture over pear filling.

To prevent overbrowning, cover edge of pie with foil. Bake in 375° oven for 25 minutes. Remove foil; bake for 25 to 30 minutes more or till pie is bubbly and crust is golden. Cool on rack before serving. Garnish with cheese triangles, if desired.

Pear-Lemon Pie

2 beaten eggs
1 cup sugar
1 teaspoon finely shredded lemon peel
¼ cup lemon juice
1 tablespoon butter *or* margarine
Pastry for Double-Crust Pie (see recipe, page 87)
1 29-ounce can *and* 1 16-ounce can pear halves, drained and cut up

In small saucepan combine the beaten eggs, sugar, lemon peel, lemon juice, and butter or margarine. Cook over low heat, stirring constantly, for 3 to 4 minutes or till thickened and bubbly. Remove from heat.

Prepare and roll out pastry. Line a 9-inch pie plate with *half* of the pastry. Trim pastry to edge of pie plate. Fold pears into thickened lemon mixture; turn into pastry-lined pie plate. Cut slits in top crust; place pastry atop filling. Seal and flute edge. To prevent overbrowning, cover edge of pie with foil. Bake in 375° oven for 20 minutes. Remove foil and bake for 25 to 30 minutes more or till golden. Cool on rack before serving.

For two dazzling desserts, drizzle warm brandied raspberry sauce over *Pear Dumplings Melba.* Or treat guests to *Strawberry Tarts* piled high with fresh strawberries and whipped cream.

Pear Dumplings Melba

6 small fresh pears
Pastry for Double-Crust Pie
  (see recipe, page 87)
6 tablespoons packed brown
  sugar
Ground cinnamon
Milk
1 tablespoon cornstarch
1 tablespoon sugar
1 10-ounce package frozen red
  raspberries, thawed
3 tablespoons brandy

Peel and core whole pears. Prepare pastry. On a lightly floured surface, roll pastry to a 21x14-inch rectangle. Cut into six 7-inch squares. Place a pear in center of each pastry square. Place *1 tablespoon* brown sugar in center of *each* pear; generously sprinkle some cinnamon atop pears.

Moisten edges of pastry with water. Fold corners to center; pinch edges together. Carefully lift dumplings into a greased 13x9x2-inch baking pan. Brush with milk. Bake in 375° oven about 40 minutes or till golden.

Meanwhile, in saucepan combine cornstarch and sugar; stir in raspberries. Cook and stir till thickened and bubbly. Press mixture through sieve to remove seeds; keep warm. To serve, in a small saucepan heat brandy. Ignite brandy and pour atop warm raspberry sauce. Stir when flame dies; spoon sauce over dumplings. Makes 6 dumplings.

Pear-Cranberry Pie

Pastry for Double-Crust Pie
  (see recipe, page 87)
½ cup sugar
3 tablespoons all-purpose flour
⅛ teaspoon ground cloves
1 16-ounce can whole cranberry
  sauce
1 tablespoon lemon juice
3 cups sliced, peeled fresh pears
  or 1 29-ounce can pear halves,
  drained and sliced
1 tablespoon butter *or* margarine

Prepare and roll out the pastry. Line a 9-inch pie plate with *half* of the pastry. Trim pastry to ¼ inch beyond edge of pie plate.

In mixing bowl combine sugar, flour, cloves, and dash *salt*. Stir in cranberry sauce and lemon juice; mix thoroughly. Gently stir in sliced pears. Turn pear-cranberry mixture into pastry-lined pie plate. Dot with butter. Cut remaining pastry into ½-inch-wide strips. Weave strips atop filling to make lattice crust; flute edge. Sprinkle top lightly with some sugar, if desired. To prevent overbrowning, cover edge of pastry with foil. Bake in 375° oven for 30 minutes. Remove foil; bake for 25 to 30 minutes more or till crust is golden. Cool pie on rack before serving.

Strawberry Tarts

Pastry for Single-Crust Pie
  (see recipe, page 84)
3 cups fresh strawberries
1 cup sugar
2 teaspoons cornstarch
1 3-ounce package
  strawberry-flavored gelatin
1 tablespoon butter *or* margarine
1 tablespoon lemon juice
Unsweetened whipped cream

Prepare and roll out pastry to a 13½x9-inch rectangle; cut into six 4½-inch squares. Fit over 6 inverted 6-ounce custard cups, pinching pleats at intervals so pastry will fit around custard cups. Prick with fork; place custard cups on baking sheet. Bake in 475° oven for 8 to 10 minutes or till golden; cool on rack.

Slice *2 cups* of the berries; set aside. In saucepan combine sugar and cornstarch. Mash remaining 1 cup of berries; add enough water to mashed berries to make 2 cups mixture. Stir into sugar mixture. Cook and stir till bubbly; cook 2 minutes more. Remove from heat. Add gelatin, butter, and lemon juice; stir till gelatin dissolves. Sieve mixture, discarding pulp. Chill till partially set. Fold in sliced berries. If necessary, chill again till mixture mounds. Spoon mixture into tart shells (shells will be very full). Chill. To serve, top with a dollop of whipped cream; garnish with additional strawberries, if desired. Cover; chill to store. Makes 6 tarts.

Strawberry Glacé Pie

Pastry for Single-Crust Pie
(see recipe, page 84)
6 cups medium fresh
strawberries
1 cup water
¾ cup sugar
3 tablespoons cornstarch
5 drops red food coloring
(optional)
Unsweetened whipped cream
(optional)

Prepare and roll out pastry. Line a 9-inch pie plate. Trim pastry to ½ inch beyond edge of pie plate. Flute edge; prick pastry. Bake in 450° oven for 10 to 12 minutes or till golden. Cool on wire rack.

To prepare strawberry glaze, in small saucepan crush *1 cup* of the smaller berries; add the water. Bring to boiling; simmer 2 minutes. Sieve berry mixture. In saucepan combine sugar and cornstarch; stir in sieved berry mixture. Cook over medium heat, stirring constantly, till strawberry glaze is thickened and clear. Stir in red food coloring, if desired.

Spread about ¼ *cup* of the strawberry glaze over bottom and sides of cooled pastry shell. Arrange *half* of the whole strawberries, stem end down, in pastry shell. Carefully spoon *half* of the remaining glaze over berries, being sure each berry is well-covered. Arrange remaining strawberries, stem end down, atop first layer; spoon on remaining glaze, covering each berry. Chill pie at least 3 to 4 hours. If desired, garnish with whipped cream.

Fresh Pineapple Pie

¾ cup sugar
3 tablespoons quick-cooking
tapioca
Dash salt
4 cups fresh pineapple cut into
¾-inch pieces
1 tablespoon lemon juice
Pastry for Double-Crust Pie
(see recipe, page 87)
1 tablespoon butter *or* margarine

In mixing bowl stir together sugar, tapioca, and salt. Add pineapple pieces and lemon juice. Let stand 15 minutes.

Prepare and roll out pastry. Line a 9-inch pie plate with *half* of the pastry. Trim pastry to edge of pie plate. Turn pineapple mixture into pastry-lined pie plate. Dot with butter or margarine. Cut slits in top crust; place atop filling. Seal and flute edge. To prevent overbrowning, cover edge of pie with foil. Bake in 375° oven for 20 minutes. Remove foil and bake for 25 to 30 minutes more or till crust is golden. Cool pie thoroughly on rack before serving.

Pineapple-Pear Cheese Pie

Pastry for Single-Crust Pie
(see recipe, page 84)
1 16-ounce can pear halves
1 20-ounce can crushed
pineapple
¼ cup sugar
2 tablespoons quick-cooking
tapioca
1 cup shredded American cheese
(4 ounces)
¼ teaspoon vanilla
Dash ground ginger
½ cup dairy sour cream
1 tablespoon sifted powdered
sugar
3 slices American cheese,
cut into triangles

Prepare and roll out pastry. Line a 9-inch pie plate. Trim pastry to ½ inch beyond edge of pie plate. Flute edge; do not prick. Bake in 450° oven for 5 minutes. Cool on wire rack. Drain pears, reserving ½ cup syrup; cut pears into 1-inch pieces. Drain pineapple, reserving ½ cup syrup. In saucepan combine reserved pear and pineapple syrups, sugar, and tapioca. Let stand for 15 minutes. Cook and stir over medium heat till mixture is thickened and bubbly. Remove from heat and stir in shredded cheese, vanilla, and ginger. Stir in pears and pineapple; turn into partially baked pastry shell.

To prevent overbrowning, cover edge of pie with foil. Bake pie in 375° oven for 20 minutes. Remove foil; bake for 20 to 25 minutes more or till crust is golden. Cool pie thoroughly on rack. Serve pie at room temperature (do not chill). To serve, combine sour cream and powdered sugar; garnish pie with dollops of sour cream mixture and cheese triangles.

2 Satiny-Smooth Cream Pies

Cream pie fans will really savor the old flavor favorites—lemon, coconut, banana, and chocolate—and all the rest of our luscious cream pies. Topped with a fluffy meringue or whipped cream, these cream pies are true winners!

Lemon Meringue Pie
(see recipe, page 30)

Create a Cream Pie

Lemon Meringue Pie (pictured on page 29)

**Pastry for Single-Crust Pie
(see recipe, page 84)**
1½ **cups sugar**
3 **tablespoons cornstarch**
3 **tablespoons all-purpose flour**
Dash salt
1½ **cups water**
3 **eggs**
2 **tablespoons butter** *or* **margarine**
½ **teaspoon finely shredded
lemon peel**
⅓ **cup lemon juice**
**Meringue for Pie (see recipe,
page 90)**

Prepare and roll out pastry. Line a 9-inch pie plate. Trim pastry to ½ inch beyond edge of pie plate. Flute edge; prick pastry. Bake in 450° oven for 10 to 12 minutes or till golden. Cool thoroughly on rack.

1 For filling, in medium saucepan combine sugar, cornstarch, flour, and salt. Gradually stir in water. **2** Cook and stir over medium-high heat till thickened and bubbly. Reduce heat; cook and stir 2 minutes more. Remove from heat.

3 Separate egg yolks from whites; set whites aside for meringue. Beat egg yolks slightly. Stir about *1 cup* of the hot mixture into the beaten yolks. **4-5** Return mixture to saucepan. Bring mixture to gentle boil. Cook and stir 2 minutes more. **6-7** Remove from heat. Stir in butter or margarine and lemon peel. Gradually stir in lemon juice, mixing well. Turn filling into baked pastry shell.

8 Make Meringue for Pie using the reserved egg whites. Spread meringue over hot filling; seal to edge. Bake in 350° oven for 12 to 15 minutes or till meringue is golden. Cool on rack. Cover; chill to store.

1

For filling, in medium saucepan combine the sugar, cornstarch, flour, and salt. Blend flour and cornstarch thoroughly with the sugar so that the starch particles are separated by sugar. This helps prevent lumps from forming when the liquid is added.

Gradually stir in the water till liquid and dry ingredients are well-mixed.

2

Cook and stir over medium-high heat till thickened and bubbly. Mixture will bubble over entire surface. Reduce heat; cook and stir 2 minutes more so the starch will cook thoroughly and filling won't taste starchy. Stir constantly while cooking so filling doesn't scorch. Remove from heat.

3

Separate egg yolks from whites; reserve whites for meringue.

In a medium bowl beat egg yolks slightly. Gradually pour *about 1 cup* of the hot mixture from the saucepan into the beaten yolks; stir constantly.

This step gradually warms the yolks before they are added to the hot mixture. If eggs are added directly to a hot mixture, they often curdle.

4

Immediately return all of the warmed egg yolk mixture to the hot filling mixture in the saucepan. The egg yolks help thicken the mixture and add richness to the filling.

5

Bring mixture to gentle boil. Cook the mixture 2 minutes more, stirring constantly with a wooden spoon. This thoroughly cooks the egg yolks. Remove saucepan from heat.

Avoid cooking the filling too long. Thickeners tend to lose some of their strength with excessive heating. If cooked too much at this point, the filling may become thin when the meringue is baked.

6

Add the butter or margarine and the lemon peel to the hot mixture in the saucepan, stirring to thoroughly combine. Gradually stir in the lemon juice, mixing well.

The lemon juice must be added last, since the acid in lemon juice can decrease the thickening power of the starch and curdle the egg.

7

Turn the hot lemon filling mixture from the saucepan into the baked pastry shell. Use a rubber spatula or wooden spoon to guide the mixture into the pastry shell.

8

Prepare meringue, referring to steps 1-4 on page 90. Immediately spread the meringue over the hot filling. Spread meringue from the edges to the center, carefully sealing to edge of crust. This contact prevents shrinkage of the meringue during baking.

Bake in 350° oven for 12 to 15 minutes or till meringue is golden. Cool on rack. Cover; chill to store.

Pie-Making Tips

• The filling for a cream pie is cooked before it goes into a baked pastry shell.
• After cooling pies to room temperature, cover and refrigerate any with fillings containing eggs or dairy products.
• To cover a meringue-topped pie, insert several toothpicks halfway into the surface of the meringue to hold wrap away from pie. Loosely cover with clear plastic wrap and chill to store. (After the meringue is refrigerated, it will be somewhat rubbery.)
• Dip a knife in water before cutting a meringue-topped pie to prevent sticking (no need to dry knife). Repeat whenever meringue sticks.

Vanilla Cream Pie

**Pastry for Single-Crust Pie
(see recipe, page 84)**
1 cup sugar
**½ cup all-purpose flour or ¼ cup
cornstarch**
¼ teaspoon salt
3 cups milk
4 eggs
3 tablespoons butter or margarine
1½ teaspoons vanilla
**Meringue for Pie (see recipe,
page 90)**

Prepare and roll out pastry. Line a 9-inch pie plate. Trim pastry to ½ inch beyond edge. Flute edge; prick pastry. Bake in 450° oven for 10 to 12 minutes or till pastry is golden. Cool thoroughly on rack.

For filling, in medium saucepan combine the sugar, flour or cornstarch, and salt. Gradually stir in milk. Cook and stir the mixture till thickened and bubbly. Reduce heat; cook and stir 2 minutes more. Remove the saucepan from heat.

Separate egg yolks from whites; set whites aside for meringue. Beat egg yolks slightly. Gradually stir *1 cup* of the hot mixture into yolks. Return egg mixture to saucepan; bring to gentle boil. Cook and stir 2 minutes more. Remove from heat. Stir in butter or margarine and the vanilla. Pour hot mixture into baked pastry shell.

Make Meringue for Pie using the 4 reserved egg whites. Spread the meringue over hot filling; seal to edge. Bake in 350° oven for 12 to 15 minutes or till meringue is golden. Cool. Cover; chill to store.

Dark Chocolate Cream Pie: Prepare Vanilla Cream Pie as directed above *except* increase sugar to *1¼ cups.* Chop 3 squares (3 ounces) *unsweetened chocolate;* add to filling along with milk.

Coconut Cream Pie

**Pastry for Single-Crust Pie
(see recipe, page 84)**
1 cup sugar
**½ cup all-purpose flour or ¼ cup
cornstarch**
¼ teaspoon salt
3 cups milk
4 eggs
3 tablespoons butter or margarine
1½ teaspoons vanilla
**1 3½-ounce can (1⅓ cups) flaked
coconut**
**Meringue for Pie (see recipe,
page 90)**

Prepare and roll out pastry. Line a 9-inch pie plate. Trim pastry to ½ inch beyond edge. Flute edge; prick pastry. Bake in 450° oven for 10 to 12 minutes or till golden. Cool thoroughly on rack.

For filling, in saucepan combine sugar, flour or cornstarch, and salt. Gradually stir in milk. Cook and stir the mixture till thickened and bubbly. Reduce heat; cook and stir 2 minutes more. Remove saucepan from heat.

Separate egg yolks from whites; set whites aside for meringue. Beat egg yolks slightly. Gradually stir *1 cup* of the hot mixture into yolks. Return egg mixture to saucepan; bring to gentle boil. Cook and stir 2 minutes more. Remove from heat. Stir in butter or margarine and vanilla. Stir in *1 cup* of the coconut. Pour hot mixture into baked pastry shell.

Make Meringue for Pie using the 4 reserved egg whites. Spread the meringue over hot filling; seal to edge. Sprinkle meringue with the remaining coconut. Bake in 350° oven for 12 to 15 minutes or till meringue is golden. Cool. Cover; chill to store.

Banana Cream Pie: Prepare Coconut Cream Pie as directed above *except* omit the flaked coconut. Slice 3 *bananas* into bottom of baked pastry shell. Pour hot cream filling mixture over bananas and top with the meringue.

Swirl fluffy meringue atop luscious *Coconut Cream Pie* and sprinkle with flaked coconut.
Then, bake the pie for a few minutes to toast the coconut and lightly brown the meringue.

Peanut Butter Pie

**Pastry for Single-Crust Pie
(see recipe, page 84)**
½ **cup sugar**
½ **cup all-purpose flour** *or* ¼ **cup
cornstarch**
¼ **teaspoon salt**
3 **cups milk**
4 **eggs**
¼ **cup creamy peanut butter**
¼ **cup coarsely chopped peanuts
(optional)**
**Meringue for Pie (see recipe,
page 90)**

Prepare and roll out pastry. Line a 9-inch pie plate. Trim pastry to ½ inch beyond edge. Flute edge; prick pastry. Bake in 450° oven for 10 to 12 minutes. Cool.

For filling, in saucepan combine sugar, flour or cornstarch, and salt. Gradually stir in milk. Cook and stir till thickened and bubbly. Reduce heat; cook and stir 2 minutes more. Remove saucepan from heat.

Separate egg yolks from whites; set whites aside for meringue. Beat yolks slightly. Gradually stir *1 cup* of the hot mixture into yolks. Return mixture to saucepan; bring to gentle boil. Cook and stir 2 minutes more. Remove saucepan from heat. Stir in peanut butter till smooth. Stir in peanuts, if desired. Pour hot mixture into baked pastry shell.

Make Meringue for Pie using the 4 reserved egg whites. Spread meringue over filling; seal to edge. Bake in 350° oven for 12 to 15 minutes. Cool. Cover; chill to store.

Milk Chocolate Pie

**Pastry for Single-Crust Pie
(see recipe, page 84)**
¾ **cup sugar**
5 **tablespoons cornstarch**
Dash salt
2½ **cups milk**
3 **squares (3 ounces) semisweet
chocolate, melted**
3 **eggs**
2 **tablespoons butter** *or* **margarine**
2 **teaspoons vanilla**
**Meringue for Pie (see recipe,
page 90)**

Prepare and roll out pastry. Line a 9-inch pie plate. Trim pastry to ½ inch beyond edge. Flute edge; prick pastry. Bake in 450° oven for 10 to 12 minutes. Cool.

For filling, in saucepan combine sugar, cornstarch, and salt. Gradually stir in milk. Cook and stir till bubbly. Reduce heat; cook and stir 2 minutes more. Stir in chocolate. Remove from heat. Separate egg yolks from whites; set whites aside for meringue. Beat yolks slightly.

Gradually stir *1 cup* of the hot mixture into yolks. Return mixture to saucepan; bring to gentle boil. Cook and stir 2 minutes more. Stir in butter or margarine and vanilla. Turn hot filling into baked pastry shell.

Make Meringue for Pie using 3 reserved egg whites. Spread meringue over filling; seal to edge. Bake in 350° oven for 12 to 15 minutes. Cool. Cover; chill to store.

Pineapple Cream Pie

**Pastry for Single-Crust Pie
(see recipe, page 84)**
½ **cup sugar**
¼ **cup all-purpose flour** *or* 2
tablespoons cornstarch
¼ **teaspoon salt**
1 **20-ounce can crushed
pineapple**
1 **cup dairy sour cream**
1 **tablespoon lemon juice**
3 **eggs**
**Meringue for Pie (see recipe,
page 90)**

Prepare and roll out pastry. Line a 9-inch pie plate. Trim pastry to ½ inch beyond edge. Flute edge; prick pastry. Bake in a 450° oven for 10 to 12 minutes. Cool.

For filling, in saucepan combine sugar, flour or cornstarch, and salt. Stir in *undrained* pineapple, sour cream, and lemon juice; mix well. Cook and stir till thickened and bubbly. Reduce heat; cook and stir 2 minutes more. Remove saucepan from heat. Separate egg yolks from whites; set whites aside for meringue. Beat egg yolks slightly. Gradually stir *1 cup* of the hot mixture into yolks. Return mixture to saucepan; bring to gentle boil. Cook and stir 2 minutes more. Pour hot mixture into baked pastry shell.

Make Meringue for Pie using the 3 reserved egg whites. Spread meringue over hot filling; seal to edge. Bake in 350° oven for 12 to 15 minutes. Cool. Cover; chill to store.

Strawberry-Pineapple Cream Pie

**Pastry for Single-Crust Pie
(see recipe, page 84)**
1 **3-*or* 3⅛-ounce package *regular*
vanilla pudding mix**
1¼ **cups milk**
1 **8¼-ounce can crushed
pineapple**
1 **teaspoon vanilla**
½ **cup whipping cream**
3 **cups fresh strawberries**
2 **tablespoons sugar**
2 **teaspoons cornstarch**
Red food coloring (optional)
Unsweetened whipped cream

Prepare and roll out pastry. Line a 9-inch pie plate. Trim pastry to ½-inch beyond edge. Flute edge; prick pastry. Bake in a 450° oven for 10 to 12 minutes or till golden. Cool on rack.

For filling, in saucepan cook pudding mix according to package directions *except* use the 1¼ cups milk. Thoroughly drain pineapple; reserve ⅓ cup liquid. Set liquid aside. Fold drained pineapple and vanilla into cooked pudding. Cover surface with clear plastic wrap or waxed paper. Cool to room temperature; do not stir. Whip the ½ cup whipping cream till soft peaks form. Fold whipped cream into pudding mixture. Turn the pineapple mixture into baked pastry shell.

In saucepan crush ½ *cup* of the strawberries; stir in reserved pineapple liquid. Bring to a boil; reduce heat and simmer for 2 minutes. Press hot mixture through sieve; discard pulp. Combine sugar and cornstarch; gradually stir in sieved strawberry mixture. Return mixture to saucepan; cook and stir till thickened and bubbly. Tint the strawberry mixture with a little red food coloring, if desired.

Slice remaining strawberries in half lengthwise. Arrange sliced berries over cream filling; spoon strawberry mixture over. Cover; chill several hours. To serve, garnish pie with unsweetened whipped cream.

Strawberry Cream Pie

**Pastry for Single-Crust Pie
(see recipe, page 84)**
⅔ **cup sugar**
3 **tablespoons cornstarch**
¼ **teaspoon salt**
2 **cups milk**
3 **eggs**
2 **tablespoons butter *or* margarine**
1 **teaspoon vanilla**
1 **10-ounce package frozen sliced
strawberries, thawed**
4 **teaspoons cornstarch**
**Meringue for Pie (see recipe,
page 90)**

Prepare and roll out pastry. Line a 9-inch pie plate. Trim pastry to ½ inch beyond edge. Flute edge; prick pastry. Bake in 450° oven for 10 to 12 minutes or till golden. Cool on rack.

For filling, in saucepan combine sugar, the 3 tablespoons cornstarch, and salt. Gradually stir in milk. Cook and stir mixture till thickened and bubbly. Reduce heat; cook and stir 2 minutes more. Remove saucepan from heat. Separate egg yolks from whites; set whites aside for meringue. Beat egg yolks slightly.

Gradually stir *1 cup* of the hot mixture into yolks. Return mixture to saucepan; bring to gentle boil. Cook and stir 2 minutes more. Remove from heat. Stir in butter or margarine and vanilla. Pour hot mixture into baked pastry shell. Cover surface with plastic wrap or waxed paper. Set vanilla filling aside to cool.

Meanwhile, in saucepan combine sliced strawberries and the 4 teaspoons cornstarch. Cook and stir till thickened and bubbly. Cook and stir 2 minutes more. Remove saucepan from heat. Cover surface with clear plastic wrap or waxed paper. Cool to room temperature. Spread cooled strawberry mixture atop vanilla filling.

Make Meringue for Pie using the 3 reserved egg whites. Spread the meringue over strawberry layer; seal to edge. Bake in 350° oven for 12 to 15 minutes or till meringue is golden. Cool. Cover; chill to store.

Lime Sour Cream Pie

Pastry for Single-Crust Pie
   (see recipe, page 84)
1   cup sugar
½   cup all-purpose flour *or* ¼ cup
      cornstarch
⅛   teaspoon salt
2   cups milk
3   eggs
¼   cup butter *or* margarine
1½   to 2 teaspoons finely shredded
      lime peel
¼   cup lime juice
½   cup dairy sour cream
   Meringue for Pie (see recipe,
      page 90)

Prepare and roll out pastry. Line a 9-inch pie plate. Trim pastry to ½ inch beyond edge. Flute edge; prick pastry. Bake in a 450° oven for 10 to 12 minutes. Cool.

For filling, in saucepan combine sugar, flour or cornstarch, and salt. Gradually stir in milk. Cook and stir till thickened and bubbly. Reduce heat; cook and stir 2 minutes more. Remove from heat. Separate egg yolks from whites; set whites aside for meringue. Beat egg yolks slightly. Gradually stir *1 cup* of the hot mixture into yolks. Return mixture to saucepan; bring to gentle boil. Cook and stir 2 minutes more. Remove saucepan from heat. Stir in butter or margarine, lime peel, and lime juice. Fold in sour cream. Turn hot lime cream filling into baked pastry shell.

Make Meringue for Pie using the 3 reserved egg whites. Spread meringue over hot filling; seal to edge. Bake in 350° oven for 12 to 15 minutes. Cool. Cover; chill to store.

Marmalade Meringue Pie

Pastry for Single-Crust Pie
   (see recipe, page 84)
½   cup sugar
3   tablespoons cornstarch
3   tablespoons all-purpose flour
   Dash salt
1½   cups water
½   cup orange marmalade
3   eggs
2   tablespoons butter *or* margarine
2   tablespoons lemon juice
   Meringue for Pie (see recipe,
      page 90)

Prepare and roll out pastry. Line a 9-inch pie plate. Trim pastry to ½ inch beyond edge. Flute edge; prick pastry. Bake in 450° oven for 10 to 12 minutes. Cool.

For filling, in saucepan combine sugar, cornstarch, flour, and salt. Gradually stir in water. Add marmalade; cook and stir till thickened and bubbly. Reduce heat; cook and stir 2 minutes more. Remove from heat. Separate egg yolks from whites; set whites aside for meringue. Beat egg yolks slightly. Stir *1 cup* of the hot mixture into yolks. Return mixture to pan; bring to gentle boil. Cook and stir 2 minutes more. Remove from heat. Stir in butter; stir in lemon juice. Pour hot mixture into baked pastry shell.

Make Meringue for Pie using the 3 reserved egg whites. Spread meringue over hot filling; seal to edge. Bake in 350° oven for 12 to 15 minutes. Cool. Cover; chill to store.

Orange Meringue Pie

Pastry for Single-Crust Pie
   (see recipe, page 84)
¾   cup sugar
¼   cup cornstarch
¼   teaspoon salt
1½   teaspoons finely shredded
      orange peel (set aside)
2   cups orange juice
3   eggs
2   tablespoons butter *or* margarine
   Meringue for Pie (see recipe,
      page 90)

Prepare and roll out pastry. Line a 9-inch pie plate. Trim pastry to ½ inch beyond edge. Flute edge; prick pastry. Bake in 450° oven for 10 to 12 minutes. Cool.

For filling, in saucepan combine sugar, cornstarch, and salt. Gradually stir in orange juice. Cook and stir till bubbly. Reduce heat; cook and stir 2 minutes more. Remove from heat. Separate egg yolks from whites; set whites aside for meringue. Beat egg yolks slightly. Gradually stir *1 cup* of the hot mixture into yolks. Return mixture to saucepan; bring to gentle boil. Cook and stir 2 minutes more. Remove saucepan from heat. Stir in butter or margarine and orange peel. Pour hot mixture into baked pastry.

Make Meringue for Pie using the 3 reserved egg whites. Spread the meringue over the hot filling; seal to edge. Bake pie in 350° oven for 12 to 15 minutes or till meringue is golden. Cool. Cover; chill to store.

Banana-Apricot Pie

Pastry for Single-Crust Pie
(see recipe, page 84)
2 cups dried apricots, snipped
1½ cups water
1¼ cups sugar
¼ cup all-purpose flour
¼ teaspoon salt
3 eggs
2 tablespoons butter *or* margarine
2 medium bananas, thinly sliced
Meringue for Pie (see recipe, page 90)

Prepare and roll out pastry. Line a 9-inch pie plate. Trim pastry to ½ inch beyond edge. Flute edge; prick pastry. Bake in 450° oven for 10 to 12 minutes. Cool.

For filling, in saucepan combine apricots and water. Cover and simmer 10 minutes or till tender. Combine sugar, flour, and salt; stir into apricot mixture. Cook and stir till thickened and bubbly. Reduce heat; cook and stir 2 minutes more. Remove from heat. Separate egg yolks from whites; set whites aside for meringue. Beat egg yolks slightly. Gradually stir *1 cup* of the hot mixture into yolks. Return mixture to saucepan; bring to gentle boil. Cook and stir 2 minutes more. Remove from heat. Stir in butter. Arrange bananas in baked pastry shell; pour hot apricot mixture atop.

Make Meringue for Pie using the 3 reserved egg whites. Spread meringue over hot filling; seal to edge. Bake in 350° oven for 12 to 15 minutes. Cool. Cover; chill to store.

Lemonade Meringue Pie

Pastry for Single-Crust Pie
(see recipe, page 84)
3 eggs
1 cup dairy sour cream
1 4½- *or* 5-ounce package *regular* vanilla pudding mix
1¼ cups milk
⅓ cup frozen lemonade concentrate, thawed
Meringue for Pie (see recipe, page 90)

Prepare and roll out pastry. Line a 9-inch pie plate. Trim pastry to ½ inch beyond edge. Flute edge; prick pastry. Bake in a 450° oven for 10 to 12 minutes. Cool.

Separate egg yolks from whites; set whites aside for meringue. For filling, in saucepan beat egg yolks slightly; add sour cream and vanilla pudding mix, stirring to mix well. Stir in milk and thawed lemonade concentrate. Cook and stir till thickened and bubbly. Pour hot lemonade mixture into baked pastry shell.

Make Meringue for Pie using the 3 reserved egg whites. Spread meringue over hot filling; seal to edge. Bake in 350° oven for 12 to 15 minutes. Cool. Cover; chill to store.

Lemon Layer Pie

Pecan Pastry for Double-Crust Pie (see recipe, page 93)
1 cup sugar
1 envelope unflavored gelatin
1¼ cups water
3 slightly beaten eggs
1 teaspoon finely shredded lemon peel
⅓ cup lemon juice
2 tablespoons butter *or* margarine
½ cup whipping cream
Unsweetened whipped cream

Prepare pastry; divide pastry in half. Roll out *one* of the portions to ⅛-inch thickness. Line a 9-inch pie plate. Trim to ½ inch beyond edge. Flute edge; prick pastry. Bake in 450° oven for 10 to 12 minutes. Cool.

Divide the remaining pastry in half. Roll out each portion to ⅛-inch thickness. Trim one to an 8-inch circle and the other to an 8¾-inch circle. Place both on a baking sheet; prick pastry. Bake in 450° oven for 8 to 10 minutes or till golden. Cool thoroughly on rack.

For filling, in saucepan combine sugar and gelatin. Stir in water, beaten eggs, lemon peel, lemon juice, and butter or margarine. Cook and stir till thickened and bubbly. Chill till mixture mounds. Whip ½ cup whipping cream till soft peaks form; fold into lemon filling.

Place *1 cup* of the lemon filling into baked pastry shell; cover with the 8-inch pastry circle. Repeat with *1 cup* lemon filling and the 8¾-inch circle. Top with remaining lemon filling. Cover and chill several hours. Garnish with unsweetened whipped cream.

Fresh Fruit Tarts

Pastry for Double-Crust Pie
   (see recipe, page 87)
⅓ cup sugar
2 tablespoons cornstarch
   Dash salt
1 cup milk
1 3-ounce package cream cheese,
      softened
2 tablespoons milk
1 slightly beaten egg yolk
½ teaspoon vanilla
1 egg white
2 tablespoons sugar
   Assorted fresh fruit
   Sugar

Prepare pastry; divide in half. Roll *half* of the pastry at a time to ⅛-inch thickness. Cut *each* half into three 5-inch circles. Fit dough circles over inverted custard cups, pinching pleats at intervals to fit around the cups; prick. Bake in 450° oven for 7 to 10 minutes or till crust is golden. Cool thoroughly.

For filling, in saucepan combine the ⅓ cup sugar, cornstarch, and salt. Gradually stir in the 1 cup milk. Cook and stir till thickened and bubbly. Remove from heat.

In small bowl combine cream cheese, the 2 tablespoons milk, and the egg yolk. Gradually stir cream cheese mixture into the hot mixture, stirring constantly. Return mixture to heat; bring to gentle boil. Cook and stir 2 minutes more. Remove from heat. Stir in vanilla. Beat egg white till soft peaks form. Gradually add the 2 tablespoons sugar, beating to stiff peaks; fold into pudding. Spoon filling into baked tart shells. Cover; chill before serving.

Prepare fruit and toss with some sugar. To serve, arrange sugared fruit atop pudding. Garnish with fresh mint leaves, chopped nuts, coconut, lemon or lime twists, or a sprinkle of ground nutmeg, if desired. Makes 6.

Strawberry Yogurt Torte

Pastry for Double-Crust Pie
   (see recipe, page 87)
1 cup strawberry yogurt
¼ cup sugar
2 cups sliced fresh strawberries
1 8½-ounce can crushed
      pineapple, well-drained
½ of a 4½-ounce container (1 cup)
      frozen whipped dessert
      topping, thawed

Prepare pastry; divide into three equal parts. Roll each portion to ⅛-inch thickness. Using a pastry wheel, trim each portion to an 8-inch circle. Place pastry circles on baking sheets; prick. Bake in 450° oven for 8 to 10 minutes or till lightly browned. Cool thoroughly.

For filling, combine yogurt and sugar; mix well. Fold in strawberries, pineapple, and dessert topping. Place one baked pastry circle on serving plate. Top with *half* of the filling; add another pastry circle. Top with remaining filling. Place remaining pastry circle atop the filling. Top with additional strawberry yogurt and strawberries, if desired. Chill at least 30 minutes. (An electric knife makes cutting into serving-size pieces easier.)

Quick Cherry Cream Tarts

Pastry for Double-Crust Pie
   (see recipe, page 87)
1 cup milk
1 cup dairy sour cream
¼ teaspoon almond extract
1 3½- *or* 3¾-ounce package
      instant vanilla pudding mix
1 21-ounce can cherry pie filling
2 tablespoons slivered toasted
      almonds

Prepare pastry. Roll *half* of the pastry at a time to ⅛-inch thickness. Cut *each* half into four 5-inch circles. Fit dough circles over inverted custard cups, pinching pleats at intervals to fit around cups; prick. Bake in 450° oven for 7 to 10 minutes or till golden. Cool.

For filling, combine milk, sour cream, and almond extract. Add dry pudding mix; beat with electric mixer or rotary beater at low speed for 1½ to 2 minutes or till creamy and well-blended. Spoon filling into baked tart shells. Top each with some of the cherry pie filling. Sprinkle with toasted almonds. Cover; chill to store. Makes 8.

Nothing tops off a dinner like a scrumptious fruit dessert. Serve this refreshing *Strawberry Yogurt Torte* or creamy *Fresh Fruit Tarts* as the sensational finale.

Choco-Almond Marble Pie

Chocolate Wafer Crust (see recipe, page 92)
6 tablespoons milk
¼ cup almond paste
2 squares (2 ounces) semisweet chocolate, melted and cooled
1 4½- *or* 5-ounce package *regular* vanilla pudding mix
Chocolate curls (optional)

Prepare Chocolate Wafer Crust. Press firmly onto bottom and sides of a 9-inch pie plate. Chill. In small mixer bowl add *1 tablespoon* of the milk at a time to almond paste, beating with electric mixer or rotary beater till smooth. Add the chocolate, beating till well-blended. Set aside.

In saucepan prepare vanilla pudding mix according to package directions for pie filling. Cool pudding mixture 5 minutes, stirring gently twice. Spread *1 cup* of the warm pudding mixture over bottom of chilled crust. Dot with *half* of the chocolate mixture. Spread remaining pudding mixture atop; dot with remaining chocolate mixture.

With narrow spatula, swirl gently through pie to marble. Cover; chill several hours or till firm. To serve, garnish pie with chocolate curls, if desired.

S'More Pie

Graham Cracker Crust (see recipe, page 92)
3 eggs
2 cups milk
1 4½- *or* 5-ounce package *regular* vanilla pudding mix
1 cup tiny marshmallows
½ cup milk chocolate pieces
Meringue for Pie (see recipe, page 90)

Prepare Graham Cracker Crust. Press crumb mixture firmly onto bottom and sides of a 9-inch pie plate. Bake in 375° oven for 5 to 6 minutes or till browned. Cool.

Separate egg yolks from whites; set whites aside for meringue. For filling, in saucepan beat egg yolks slightly. Stir in milk and vanilla pudding mix. Cook and stir till thickened and bubbly. Remove from heat. Cover surface with clear plastic wrap or waxed paper; cool to room temperature. Place marshmallows in baked pastry shell. Sprinkle chocolate pieces evenly over marshmallows. Spoon cooled filling over chocolate pieces.

Make Meringue for Pie using the 3 reserved egg whites. Spread the meringue over filling; seal to edge. Bake in 350° oven for 12 to 15 minutes or till meringue is golden. Cool. Cover; chill to store.

Pumpkin Meringue Pie

Pastry for Single-Crust Pie (see recipe, page 84)
¾ cup sugar
3 tablespoons cornstarch
½ teaspoon salt
½ teaspoon ground cinnamon
½ teaspoon ground ginger
¼ teaspoon ground nutmeg
⅛ teaspoon ground cloves
2 cups milk
1 cup canned pumpkin
3 eggs
Meringue for Pie (see recipe, page 90)

Prepare and roll out pastry. Line a 9-inch pie plate. Trim pastry to ½ inch beyond edge. Flute edge; prick pastry. Bake in 450° oven for 10 to 12 minutes or till crust is golden. Cool on rack.

For filling, in saucepan combine sugar, cornstarch, salt, cinnamon, ginger, nutmeg, and cloves. Gradually stir in milk and pumpkin. Cook and stir till thickened and bubbly. Reduce heat; cook and stir 2 minutes more. Remove from heat. Separate egg yolks from whites; set whites aside for meringue. Beat egg yolks slightly. Gradually stir *1 cup* of the hot mixture into yolks. Return mixture to saucepan; bring to gentle boil. Cook and stir 2 minutes more. Pour hot mixture into baked pastry shell.

Make Meringue for Pie using the 3 reserved egg whites. Spread the meringue over the hot filling; seal to edge. Bake in 350° oven for 12 to 15 minutes or till golden. Cool on rack. Cover; chill to store.

Chocolate-Cherry Cream Torte (pictured on page 4)

**Pastry for Double-Crust Pie
(see recipe, page 87)**
⅔ **cup sugar**
¼ **cup all-purpose flour or 2
tablespoons cornstarch**
⅛ **teaspoon salt**
1½ **cups milk**
1 **square (1 ounce) unsweetened
chocolate, broken into pieces**
2 **eggs**
1 **tablespoon butter or margarine**
¾ **teaspoon vanilla**
½ **teaspoon vanilla**
¼ **teaspoon cream of tartar**
¼ **cup sugar**
1 **21-ounce can cherry pie filling**

Prepare pastry and roll out to an 18x10-inch rectangle. Cut into four 9x5-inch rectangles. Carefully transfer pastry rectangles to large baking sheet; prick. Bake in 450° oven for 10 to 12 minutes or till golden. Cool.

For filling, in saucepan combine the ⅔ cup sugar, the flour or cornstarch, and salt. Gradually stir in milk; add the chocolate pieces. Cook and stir till thickened and bubbly. Reduce heat; cook and stir 2 minutes more. Remove from heat. Separate egg yolks from whites; set whites aside for meringue. Beat egg yolks slightly. Gradually stir 1 cup of the hot mixture into yolks. Return mixture to saucepan; bring to gentle boil. Cook and stir 2 minutes more. Stir in butter or margarine and ¾ teaspoon vanilla. Pour hot mixture into bowl. Cover surface with clear plastic wrap or waxed paper; cool to room temperature. Chill.

To make meringue, beat the 2 reserved egg whites with ½ teaspoon vanilla and cream of tartar till soft peaks form. Gradually add ¼ cup sugar; beat to stiff peaks. Cover; set aside.

Place one baked pastry rectangle on serving plate. Top with half of the chocolate filling, spreading evenly. Add another pastry rectangle. Top with half of the cherry pie filling and another pastry rectangle. Top with the remaining chocolate filling. Place the one remaining pastry rectangle on a baking sheet. Top with the remaining cherry pie filling. Using a star tip, pipe meringue atop cherry filling. Broil 4 to 5 inches from heat for 1 to 2 minutes or till golden. Carefully slide two wide spatulas under the pastry and place atop chocolate filling. Chill overnight before serving. (An electric knife makes cutting the torte into serving-size pieces easier.)

Chocolate Layer Pie

**Pastry for Single-Crust Pie
(see recipe, page 84)**
1 **4- or 5¼-ounce package regular
chocolate pudding mix**
1 **3½- or 3¾-ounce package
instant vanilla pudding mix**
1 **cup milk**
1 **cup dairy sour cream**
2 **tablespoons milk**
Chocolate curls

Prepare and roll out pastry. Line a 9-inch pie plate. Trim pastry to ½ inch beyond edge. Flute edge; prick pastry. Bake in 450° oven for 10 to 12 minutes or till golden. Cool thoroughly on rack.

To prepare filling, in saucepan prepare chocolate pudding according to package directions for pie filling. Cover surface with clear plastic wrap or waxed paper; cool to room temperature. Prepare vanilla pudding according to package directions for pie except use 1 cup milk; stir in sour cream. Beat mixture with electric mixer or rotary beater at low speed for 1½ to 2 minutes or till creamy and well-blended. Stir 1 cup of the prepared vanilla pudding into the cooled chocolate; stir till thoroughly mixed and smooth. Spread chocolate filling evenly in baked pastry shell. Add the 2 tablespoons milk to the remaining vanilla pudding, stirring till smooth. Immediately spread vanilla pudding over chocolate filling. Cover; chill 3 to 4 hours or overnight. Garnish pie with chocolate curls.

Quick Raisin Pudding Pie

Pastry for Single-Crust Pie
(see recipe, page 84)
½ cup hot freshly brewed coffee
1½ cups raisins
½ teaspoon ground cinnamon
Dash cloves
1 3½- *or* 3¾-ounce package
instant vanilla pudding mix
1¼ cups milk
½ cup coarsely chopped walnuts

Prepare and roll out pastry. Line a 9-inch pie plate. Trim to ½ inch beyond edge. Flute edge; prick pastry. Bake in 450° oven for 10 to 12 minutes or till golden. Cool thoroughly on rack.

In small bowl pour hot coffee over raisins. Stir in cinnamon and cloves; let stand for 10 minutes.

For filling, prepare pudding mix according to directions for pie filling *except* use 1¼ cups milk. Beat mixture with electric mixer or rotary beater at low speed for 1½ to 2 minutes or till well-blended. Stir in raisin mixture. Turn filling into baked pastry. Cover; chill till cooled. Garnish with chopped nuts.

Quick Apple Cream Pie

Pastry for Single-Crust Pie
(see recipe, page 84)
1 21-ounce can French apple pie
filling
1 3½- *or* 3¾-ounce package
instant vanilla pudding mix
1 cup milk
1 cup dairy sour cream
2 tablespoons sliced toasted
almonds

Prepare and roll out pastry. Line a 9-inch pie plate. Trim pastry to ½ inch beyond edge. Flute edge; prick pastry. Bake in 450° oven for 10 to 12 minutes or till golden. Cool thoroughly on rack.

Pour pie filling into baked pastry shell. Prepare vanilla pudding according to package directions for pie filling *except* use 1 cup milk; stir in sour cream. Beat mixture with electric mixer or rotary beater at low speed for 1½ to 2 minutes or till well-blended. Spread pudding mixture over the pie filling. Cover and chill. Garnish pie with toasted almonds.

Quick Lemon-Pineapple Pie

Graham Cracker Crust
(see recipe, page 92)
1 20-ounce can crushed
pineapple
1 3½- *or* 3¾-ounce package
instant lemon pudding
mix
1 envelope dessert topping mix

Prepare Graham Cracker Crust. Press crumb mixture firmly onto bottom and sides of a 9-inch pie plate. Chill. For filling, in bowl stir together *undrained* pineapple and dry pudding mix. Prepare topping mix following package directions; fold into pineapple mixture. Turn into the chilled crust. Cover; chill pie. Garnish pie with more whipped dessert topping, if desired.

Quick Mince Cream Pie

Pastry for Single-Crust Pie
(see recipe, page 84)
1 28-ounce jar prepared
mincemeat
1 3½- *or* 3¾-ounce package
instant vanilla pudding mix
1½ cups milk
1 teaspoon finely shredded
orange peel
⅛ teaspoon ground nutmeg

Prepare and roll out pastry. Line a 9-inch pie plate. Trim pastry to ½ inch beyond edge. Flute edge; prick pastry. Bake in 450° oven for 10 to 12 minutes or till golden. Cool thoroughly on rack. Spoon the mincemeat into baked pastry shell.

For filling, prepare vanilla pudding mix according to package directions for pie filling *except* use 1½ cups milk; stir in orange peel and nutmeg. Beat mixture with electric mixer or rotary beater at low speed for 1½ to 2 minutes or till creamy and well-blended. Spread filling over mincemeat. Cover and chill to store.

3 Classy Custard Pies

Custard pies lend themselves to many delicious variations. Pumpkin Pie, Pecan Pie, and Lemon-Chess Pie are all custard types. Be sure to try these favorites as well as the traditional custard pies.

Pumpkin Pie
(see recipe, page 44)

Create a Custard Pie

Pumpkin Pie (pictured on page 43)

Pastry for Single-Crust Pie
(see recipe, page 84)
1 **16-ounce can pumpkin**
¾ **cup sugar**
1 **teaspoon ground cinnamon**
½ **teaspoon salt**
½ **teaspoon ground ginger**
½ **teaspoon ground nutmeg**
3 **eggs**
1 **5⅓-ounce can (⅔ cup)**
   evaporated milk
½ **cup milk**
   Unsweetened whipped cream
   (optional)

Prepare and roll out pastry. Line a 9-inch pie plate. Trim pastry to ½ inch beyond edge of pie plate. Flute edge high; do not prick pastry.

1 In large mixing bowl combine pumpkin, sugar, cinnamon, salt, ginger, and nutmeg. **2-3** Add eggs; lightly beat eggs into pumpkin mixture with a fork. **4** Add the evaporated milk and milk; mix well. **5** Place pie shell on oven rack; pour mixture into the pastry-lined pie plate. **6** To prevent overbrowning, cover edge of pie with foil. Bake in 375° oven for 25 minutes. Remove foil; bake for 25 to 30 minutes more or till knife inserted off-center comes out clean. Cool thoroughly on rack before serving. Garnish with dollops of unsweetened whipped cream, if desired. Cover and chill to store.

Honey-Pumpkin Pie: Omit the ¾ cup sugar and add ½ cup *honey* to pumpkin mixture.

Raisin-Pumpkin Pie: Add ⅛ teaspoon *ground cloves* and ¾ cup *light raisins* to pumpkin mixture.

Molasses-Pumpkin Pie: Decrease sugar to ½ cup and add ⅓ cup *molasses* to pumpkin mixture.

1
In a large mixing bowl stir together the canned pumpkin, sugar, ground cinnamon, salt, ground ginger, and nutmeg. Mix well with a rubber spatula or wooden spoon to thoroughly combine ingredients. Stir till the pumpkin-spice mixture is smooth.

2
Add the eggs to the thoroughly mixed pumpkin-spice mixture. To avoid mixing any eggshell into the pumpkin mixture, carefully break each egg into a custard cup or small bowl; skim off any shell fragments before adding the egg to the pumpkin mixture.

3

Lightly beat the eggs into the pumpkin-spice mixture with a fork until thoroughly blended. (The eggs cause the pie filling to thicken as it bakes.) It is not necessary to vigorously beat air into the pumpkin mixture, as this recipe makes a very full pie

4

Add the evaporated milk and the milk to the pumpkin-egg mixture; stir till well-combined. The milk is added last so that the pumpkin mixture will be easier to handle. Once the milk is added, the mixture becomes very thin and is easily splashed when poured into the pastry-lined pie plate.

5

Be sure the pastry in the pie plate has high fluted edges, since this recipe makes a very full pie. Place pastry-lined pie plate on oven rack; fill. Pour pumpkin filling directly from bowl, or transfer mixture to a large measuring cup or pitcher. This helps prevent accidental spilling of the pie filling.

6

To prevent overbrowning, cover edge of pie with foil. Bake in 375° oven for 25 minutes. Remove foil; bake for 25 to 30 minutes more or till knife inserted off-center comes out clean, as shown. Cool pie thoroughly on rack before serving. Garnish with dollops of unsweetened whipped cream, if desired. Cover; chill to store.

Pie-Making Tips

- Custard pies consist of an egg and milk mixture in which the egg cooks and thus thickens the pie during baking.
- Avoid messy spills by placing the pie shell on the oven rack, then pouring in the liquid pie filling.
- To check for doneness after baking for the recommended time, insert a knife off-center; if it comes out clean with no custard filling clinging to it, the pie is done.
- Or, gently shake the pie. If the area that appears to be liquid is less than the size of a quarter, pie is done. It will continue to set after it is removed from oven.
- Overcooking custard mixtures results in an undesirable product. When a baked custard pie overcooks, tiny bubbles appear around the edge of the pie, and there is a separation of liquid from solid when custard is cut.
- After the custard pie cools to room temperature, always cover and refrigerate it if it's to be stored for any length of time before serving. Cover and chill to store after serving, as well.

Praline Pumpkin Pie

**Pastry for Single-Crust Pie
(see recipe, page 84)**
1 **tablespoon butter *or* margarine**
½ **cup chopped pecans**
¼ **cup butter *or* margarine**
⅓ **cup packed brown sugar**
⅓ **cup granulated sugar**
1 **2¼- *or* 3-ounce package
no-bake custard mix**
2 **teaspoons pumpkin pie spice**
1 **16-ounce can (2 cups) pumpkin**
⅔ **cup milk**
1 **5⅓-ounce can (⅔ cup)
evaporated milk**
Toasted chopped pecans

Prepare and roll out pastry. Line a 9-inch pie plate. Trim pastry to ½ inch beyond edge of pie plate. Flute edge; prick pastry. Bake in 450° oven for 10 to 12 minutes or till golden. Cool thoroughly on rack.

To toast pecans, dot 1 tablespoon butter or margarine over pecans in shallow baking pan. Bake in 350° oven for 15 minutes or till toasted, stirring often. For filling, in small saucepan melt the ¼ cup butter or margarine. Stir in the brown sugar and ½ cup toasted pecans; cook and stir till bubbly. Spread over bottom of baked pastry shell; cool to room temperature. In medium saucepan combine granulated sugar, custard mix, and pumpkin pie spice. Stir in pumpkin, milk, and evaporated milk. Cook and stir till bubbly. Cover and cool 10 minutes. Carefully pour pumpkin mixture over pecans in pastry shell. Chill pie till firm before serving. Garnish top with additional toasted pecans. Cover and chill to store.

Custard Pie

**Pastry for Single-Crust Pie
(see recipe, page 84)**
4 **eggs**
½ **cup sugar**
½ **teaspoon vanilla**
¼ **teaspoon salt**
2½ **cups milk**
Ground nutmeg

Prepare and roll out pastry. Line a 9-inch pie plate. Trim to ½ inch beyond edge. Flute edge high; do not prick. Bake in 450° oven for 5 minutes. Cool on rack.

For filling, in mixing bowl beat eggs slightly with rotary beater or fork. Stir in the sugar, vanilla, and salt. Gradually stir in milk; mix well. Place pie shell on oven rack; pour filling into partially baked pastry shell. Sprinkle with a little nutmeg.

To prevent overbrowning, cover edge of pie with foil. Bake in 350° oven for 30 minutes. Remove foil; bake for 30 to 35 minutes more or till knife inserted off-center comes out clean. Cool pie on rack before serving. Cover; chill to store.

Note: If desired, omit nutmeg and sprinkle ½ cup *flaked coconut* atop unbaked filling and bake as above.

Butterscotch Custard Pie

**Pastry for Single-Crust Pie
(see recipe, page 84)**
4 **eggs**
1 **13-ounce can *and* 1 5⅓-ounce
can evaporated milk**
1 **cup packed brown sugar**
**Unsweetened whipped cream
(optional)**

Prepare and roll out pastry. Line a 9-inch pie plate. Trim pastry to ½ inch beyond edge. Flute edge high; do not prick. Bake in 450° oven for 5 minutes. Cool.

For filling, in mixing bowl beat eggs slightly with rotary beater or fork. Stir in the 2 cans of evaporated milk and brown sugar, stirring thoroughly to dissolve brown sugar. Place pie shell on oven rack; pour mixture into the partially baked pastry shell. To prevent overbrowning, cover edge of pie with foil. Bake in 350° oven for 25 minutes. Remove foil; bake for 20 to 25 minutes more or till knife inserted off-center comes out clean. Cool thoroughly on rack. Garnish pie with dollops of whipped cream, if desired. Cover; chill to store.

Note: The surface of this pie will typically appear mottled and bubbly.

Eggnog Custard Tarts (pictured on page 51)

Pastry for Double-Crust Pie
(see recipe, page 86)
4 eggs
3 cups canned *or* dairy eggnog
½ cup sugar
2 tablespoons light rum
1 teaspoon vanilla
¼ teaspoon salt
Ground nutmeg

Prepare and roll out pastry. Roll *half* of the pastry at a time to ⅛-inch thickness. Cut each half into three 6½- or 7-inch circles. Line 4½-inch tart pans with pastry. Flute edge high; do not prick pastry. Bake in 450° oven for 5 minutes. Cool on rack.

For filling, in mixing bowl beat eggs slightly with rotary beater or fork. Stir in the eggnog, sugar, light rum, vanilla, and salt; mix well. Place tart pans on baking sheet. Place sheet on oven rack; pour some filling into each partially baked tart shell. Sprinkle each tart with a little nutmeg. Bake in 350° oven about 40 minutes or till knife inserted off-center comes out clean. Cool on rack. Cover; chill to store. Makes 6 tarts.

Chocolate-Topped Custard Pie

Pastry for Single-Crust Pie
(see recipe, page 84)
4 eggs
2⅔ cups milk
⅔ cup sugar
¼ teaspoon salt
Dash ground nutmeg
¼ cup milk chocolate pieces
1 tablespoon milk
Unsweetened whipped cream
(optional)
Coarsely grated chocolate
(optional)

Prepare and roll out pastry. Line a 9-inch plate. Trim pastry to ½ inch beyond edge of pie plate. Flute edge; do not prick. Bake in 450° oven for 5 minutes. Cool.

For filling, in mixing bowl beat eggs slightly with rotary beater or fork. Stir in the 2⅔ cups milk, sugar, salt, and nutmeg; mix well. Place pie shell on oven rack; pour filling into partially baked pastry shell. To prevent overbrowning, cover edge of pie with foil. Bake in 375° oven for 20 minutes. Remove foil; bake about 25 minutes more or till knife inserted off-center comes out clean. Cool pie on rack.

In small saucepan add chocolate pieces and 1 tablespoon milk; cook and stir till chocolate is melted. Remove from heat; stir in enough additional milk till of drizzling consistency. Quickly drizzle over the cooled pie. Chill. Garnish with whipped cream and sprinkle with grated chocolate, if desired. Cover; chill to store.

Peach-Pineapple Custard Pie

Pastry for Single-Crust Pie
(see recipe, page 84)
1 21-ounce can peach pie filling
1 8¼-ounce can crushed
pineapple, drained
1 cup dairy sour cream
1 3-ounce package cream cheese,
softened
2 eggs
⅓ cup sugar

Prepare and roll out pastry. Line a 9-inch pie plate. Trim pastry to ½ inch beyond edge of pie plate. Flute edge; do not prick pastry. Bake in 450° oven for 5 minutes. Cool thoroughly on rack.

For filling, in mixing bowl combine pie filling and crushed pineapple; turn into the partially baked pastry shell. In mixer bowl with electric mixer or rotary beater, beat together sour cream and cream cheese; add eggs and sugar, beating mixture till smooth. Place pie shell on oven rack; pour sour cream-egg mixture over peach-pineapple layer. To prevent overbrowning, cover edge of pie with foil. Bake in 375° oven for 15 minutes. Remove foil; bake for 15 to 20 minutes more or till crust is golden and filling is set. Cool on rack. Cover; chill to store.

Peanut Custard Pie

Pastry for Single-Crust Pie
  (see recipe, page 84)
3 **eggs**
1 **cup dark corn syrup**
⅔ **cup sugar**
⅓ **cup butter *or* margarine, melted**
1 **teaspoon vanilla**
  Dash salt
1 **cup peanuts**
  Unsweetened whipped cream

Prepare and roll out pastry. Line a 9-inch pie plate. Trim pastry to ½ inch beyond edge of pie plate. Flute edge; do not prick pastry. Bake in 450° oven for 5 minutes. Cool thoroughly on rack.

For filling, in mixing bowl beat eggs slightly with rotary beater. Stir in the corn syrup, sugar, butter or margarine, vanilla, and salt; beat with rotary beater till smooth. Stir in peanuts. Place pie shell on oven rack; pour mixture into the partially baked pastry shell. To prevent overbrowning, cover edge of pie with foil. Bake in 350° oven for 25 minutes. Remove foil; bake for 15 to 20 minutes more or till knife inserted off-center comes out clean. Cool pie on rack before serving. Garnish pie with whipped cream. Cover; chill to store.

Raisin-Coconut Pie

Pastry for Single-Crust Pie
  (see recipe, page 84)
½ **cup raisins**
  Boiling water
3 **eggs**
1½ **cups sugar**
½ **cup butter *or* margarine, melted**
1 **tablespoon lemon juice**
1 **teaspoon vanilla**
½ **cup flaked coconut**
  Unsweetened whipped cream

Prepare and roll out pastry. Line a 9-inch pie plate. Trim pastry to ½ inch beyond edge of pie plate. Flute edge; do not prick pastry. Bake in 450° oven for 5 minutes. Cool thoroughly on rack.

To plump raisins, in small mixing bowl cover raisins with boiling water; let stand 5 minutes. Drain. For filling, in another mixing bowl beat eggs slightly with rotary beater or fork. Stir in sugar, melted butter or margarine, lemon juice, and vanilla; mix well. Stir in coconut and well-drained raisins.

Place pie shell on oven rack; pour filling into the partially baked pastry shell. To prevent overbrowning, cover edge of pie with foil. Bake in 350° oven for 30 minutes. Remove foil; bake for 20 to 25 minutes more or till knife inserted off-center comes out clean. Cool pie on rack before serving. Garnish with whipped cream. Cover; chill to store.

Maple-Nut Pie

Pastry for Single-Crust Pie
  (see recipe, page 84)
⅓ **cup packed brown sugar**
2 **tablespoons all-purpose flour**
3 **eggs**
1 **cup pure maple syrup *or***
  maple-flavored syrup
2 **tablespoons butter *or***
  margarine, melted
1 **teaspoon vanilla**
  Dash salt
½ **cup chopped pecans**
  Unsweetened whipped cream
  (optional)

Prepare and roll out pastry. Line a 9-inch pie plate. Trim pastry to ½ inch beyond edge of pie plate. Flute edge; do not prick pastry. Bake in 450° oven for 5 minutes. Cool thoroughly on rack.

For filling, combine brown sugar and flour. In mixing bowl beat eggs slightly with rotary beater or fork. Stir in sugar-flour mixture, maple syrup or maple-flavored syrup, melted butter or margarine, vanilla, and salt; beat with rotary beater just till smooth. Stir in pecans.

Place pie shell on oven rack; pour filling into the partially baked pastry shell. To prevent overbrowning, cover edge of pie with foil. Bake in 350° oven for 25 minutes. Remove foil; bake for 15 to 20 minutes more or till knife inserted off-center comes out clean. Cool pie thoroughly on rack before serving. Garnish with whipped cream, if desired. Cover; chill to store.

Holiday Nut Pie

Pastry for Single-Crust Pie
(see recipe, page 84)
3 eggs
⅓ cup granulated sugar
½ cup packed brown sugar
½ cup light cream *or* milk
¼ cup butter *or* margarine, melted
¼ cup light corn syrup
½ teaspoon vanilla
¼ teaspoon salt
1 cup coarsely chopped walnuts
Unsweetened whipped cream
(optional)

Prepare and roll out pastry. Line a 9-inch pie plate. Trim pastry to ½ inch beyond edge of pie plate. Flute edge; do not prick pastry. Bake in 450° oven for 5 minutes. Cool thoroughly on rack.

For filling, in mixing bowl beat eggs slightly with rotary beater or fork. Stir in granulated sugar, brown sugar, light cream or milk, melted butter or margarine, corn syrup, vanilla, and salt; mix well. Stir in chopped walnuts. Place pie shell on oven rack; pour filling into the partially baked pastry shell. To prevent overbrowning, cover edge of pie with foil. Bake in 375° oven for 20 minutes. Remove foil; bake for 15 to 20 minutes more or till knife inserted off-center comes out clean. Cool pie thoroughly on rack before serving. Garnish with whipped cream, if desired. Cover; chill to store.

Home-Style Coconut Pie

Pastry for Single-Crust Pie
(see recipe, page 84)
3 eggs
1½ cups light cream *or* milk
1 cup sugar
2 tablespoons butter *or*
margarine, melted
1½ teaspoons vanilla
1 3½-ounce can (1⅓ cups) flaked
coconut

Prepare and roll out pastry. Line a 9-inch pie plate. Trim pastry to ½ inch beyond edge of pie plate. Flute edge; do not prick. Bake in 450° oven for 5 minutes. Cool.

For filling, in mixing bowl beat eggs slightly with rotary beater or fork. Stir in light cream or milk, sugar, melted butter or margarine, and vanilla; mix well. Stir in flaked coconut. Place pie shell on oven rack; pour filling into the partially baked pastry shell. To prevent overbrowning, cover edge of pie with foil. Bake in 350° oven for 25 minutes. Remove foil; bake for 25 minutes more or till knife inserted off-center comes out clean. Cool pie on rack before serving. Cover; chill to store.

Brownie-Scotch Pie

Pastry for Single-Crust Pie
(see recipe, page 84)
1½ cups packed brown sugar
¼ cup butter *or* margarine
3 eggs
1 square (1 ounce) unsweetened
chocolate, melted and cooled
½ cup milk
1 teaspoon vanilla
Unsweetened whipped cream

Prepare and roll out pastry. Line a 9-inch pie plate. Trim pastry to ½ inch beyond edge of pie plate. Flute edge; do not prick pastry. Bake in 450° oven for 5 minutes. Cool thoroughly on rack.

For filling, in mixer bowl beat brown sugar and butter or margarine with electric mixer or rotary beater till well combined. Add eggs, one at a time, beating at low speed just till combined. Blend in cooled chocolate; stir in milk and vanilla. (Mixture may look slightly curdled.) Place pie shell on oven rack; pour filling into the partially baked pastry shell.

To prevent overbrowning, cover edge of pie with foil. Bake in 375° oven for 20 minutes. Remove foil; bake for 10 to 15 minutes more or till knife inserted off-center comes out clean. Cool pie thoroughly on rack before serving. Garnish with unsweetened whipped cream. Cover; chill pie to store.

Note: During baking, the pie filling separates into a custard layer that's topped with a brownie-like layer.

Pecan Pie

Pastry for Single-Crust Pie
  (see recipe, page 84)
3 **eggs**
⅔ **cup sugar**
  Dash salt
1 **cup dark corn syrup**
⅓ **cup butter *or* margarine, melted**
1 **cup pecan halves**

Prepare and roll out pastry. Line a 9-inch pie plate. Trim pastry to ½ inch beyond edge of pie plate. Flute edge; do not prick pastry.

For filling, in mixing bowl beat eggs slightly with rotary beater or fork. Add sugar and salt, stirring till dissolved. Stir in dark corn syrup and melted butter or margarine; mix well. Stir in the pecan halves. Place pie shell on oven rack; pour filling into the pastry-lined pie plate. To prevent overbrowning, cover edge of pie with foil. Bake in 350° oven for 25 minutes. Remove foil; bake about 25 minutes more or till knife inserted off-center comes out clean. Cool thoroughly on rack before serving. Cover; chill to store.

Cranberry-Pecan Pie: Prepare the pastry shell as above. Prepare the egg-corn syrup filling. Stir in 1 cup coarsely chopped *fresh cranberries* and the pecans. Bake as above.

Orange-Pecan Pie: Prepare the pastry shell as above. Prepare the egg-corn syrup filling. Stir in ½ teaspoon of finely shredded *orange peel,* ½ cup finely chopped *orange,* and the pecan halves. Bake as directed above.

Pecan Tassies

½ **cup butter *or* margarine,**
  softened
1 **3-ounce package cream cheese,**
  softened
1 **cup all-purpose flour**
1 **egg**
¾ **cup packed brown sugar**
1 **tablespoon butter *or* margarine,**
  softened
1 **teaspoon vanilla**
  Dash salt
½ **cup coarsely chopped pecans**

For pastry, in mixing bowl cream together the ½ cup butter or margarine and softened cream cheese. Stir in flour; mix well. Cover; chill mixture about 1 hour.

In small mixing bowl stir together egg, brown sugar, the 1 tablespoon butter or margarine, vanilla, and salt just till smooth; set aside. Shape chilled pastry dough into two dozen 1-inch balls; place each ball in *ungreased* 1¾-inch muffin cup. Press dough onto bottom and sides of cups. Spoon about *1 teaspoon* of the chopped pecans into *each* pastry-lined muffin cup; fill each with egg mixture. Bake in 325° oven about 25 minutes or till filling is set. Cool; remove from pans. Cover; chill to store. Makes 24.

Coconut-Oatmeal Pie

Pastry for Single-Crust Pie
  (see recipe, page 84)
½ **cup sugar**
¼ **cup butter *or* margarine,**
  softened
1 **cup light corn syrup**
¼ **teaspoon salt**
3 **eggs**
½ **cup flaked coconut**
½ **cup quick-cooking rolled oats**

Prepare and roll out pastry. Line a 9-inch pie plate. Trim pastry to ½ inch beyond edge of pie plate. Flute edge; do not prick pastry. Bake in 450° oven for 5 minutes. Cool thoroughly on rack.

In medium mixer bowl gradually add sugar to softened butter or margarine, beating till fluffy with electric mixer or rotary beater. Add corn syrup and salt; beat well. Add eggs, one at a time, beating till thoroughly mixed. Stir in coconut and rolled oats. Place pie shell on oven rack; pour filling into the partially baked pastry shell. To prevent overbrowning, cover edge of pie with foil. Bake in 350° oven for 30 minutes. Remove foil; bake for 15 to 20 minutes more or till knife inserted off-center comes out clean. Cool before serving. Cover; chill to store.

Any of these custard specialties is sure to please family and friends! Choose
Cranberry-Pecan Pie, Pecan Tassies, or delicate *Eggnog Custard Tarts* (see recipe, page 47).

Brown Sugar-Rhubarb Pie

Pastry for Single-Crust Pie
(see recipe, page 84)
1 to 1¼ cups packed brown sugar
¼ cup all-purpose flour
¼ teaspoon salt
4 cups diced rhubarb (1 pound)
3 eggs
1 tablespoon lemon juice
Meringue for Pie (see recipe,
page 90)

Prepare and roll out pastry. Line a 9-inch pie plate. Trim pastry to ½ inch beyond edge of pie plate. Flute edge; do not prick. Bake in 450° oven for 5 minutes. Cool.

To prepare filling, combine brown sugar, flour, and salt; stir in rhubarb. Let stand 15 minutes. Separate egg yolks from whites; set whites aside for meringue. Beat yolks slightly. Stir beaten yolks and lemon juice into rhubarb mixture. Turn rhubarb filling into partially baked pastry shell. To prevent overbrowning, cover edge of pie with foil. Bake in 375° oven for 25 minutes. Remove foil; bake for 20 to 25 minutes more or till nearly set. *(Pie appears soft in center but becomes firm after cooling.)*

Make Meringue for Pie using the 3 reserved egg whites. Spread meringue over filling; seal to edge. Bake in 350° oven for 12 to 15 minutes. Cool. Cover; chill to store.

Fig-Nut Pie

Pastry for Single-Crust Pie
(see recipe, page 84)
6 beaten eggs
1 cup sugar
3 tablespoons lemon juice
3 tablespoons butter *or*
margarine, melted
½ teaspoon ground cinnamon
½ teaspoon ground nutmeg
1½ cups chopped dried figs
1 cup chopped walnuts
Unsweetened whipped cream

Prepare and roll out pastry. Line a 9-inch pie plate with pastry. Trim pastry to ½ inch beyond edge of pie plate. Flute edge; do not prick pastry. Bake in 450° oven for 5 minutes. Cool on a wire rack.

For filling, in mixing bowl combine eggs, sugar, lemon juice, butter, cinnamon, nutmeg, and ¼ teaspoon *salt*. Stir in figs and walnuts. Pour filling into partially baked pastry shell. To prevent overbrowning, cover edge of pie with foil. Bake in 375° oven for 20 minutes. Remove foil; bake about 20 minutes more or till knife inserted off-center comes out clean. Cool before serving. Serve with whipped cream. Cover; chill to store.

Pumpkin-Apple Pie

Pastry for Single-Crust Pie
(see recipe, page 84)
½ cup packed brown sugar
½ cup water
2 tablespoons butter *or* margarine
1 tablespoon cornstarch
1 teaspoon ground cinnamon
½ teaspoon salt
4 cups sliced, peeled cooking
apples
1 tablespoon lemon juice
1 slightly beaten egg
1 cup canned pumpkin
½ cup granulated sugar
½ teaspoon ground ginger
⅛ teaspoon ground cloves
1 5⅓-ounce can (⅔ cup)
evaporated milk
Unsweetened whipped cream

Prepare and roll out pastry. Line a 9-inch pie plate. Trim pastry to ½ inch beyond edge. Flute edge high; do not prick. Bake in 450° oven for 5 minutes. Cool on rack.

For filling, in medium saucepan combine brown sugar, water, butter or margarine, cornstarch, cinnamon, and ¼ *teaspoon* of the salt. Cook and stir over medium heat till mixture comes to boiling. Stir in sliced apples. Cover and cook for 5 to 6 minutes or till apples are crisp-tender, stirring occasionally. Remove from heat; stir in lemon juice. Spread apple mixture evenly in bottom of partially baked pastry shell.

In mixing bowl combine egg, pumpkin, granulated sugar, ginger, cloves, and the remaining ¼ teaspoon salt; mix well. Stir in evaporated milk. Carefully pour pumpkin mixture over apples. To prevent overbrowning, cover edge of pie with foil. Bake in 375° oven for 20 minutes. Remove foil; bake for 20 to 25 minutes more or till knife inserted off-center comes out clean. Cool pie thoroughly on rack. Serve with whipped cream. Cover; chill to store.

Rhubarb-Raisin Pie

Pastry for Single-Crust Pie
  (see recipe, page 84)
3 eggs
¼ cup raisins
  Boiling water
1 cup sugar
2 tablespoons all-purpose flour
½ cup orange juice
3 cups chopped rhubarb
  (about 1 pound)
  Meringue for Pie (see recipe,
  page 90)

Prepare and roll out pastry. Line a 9-inch pie plate. Trim to ½ inch beyond edge. Flute edge high; do not prick. Bake in 450° oven for 5 minutes. Cool on rack.

Separate egg yolks from whites; set whites aside for meringue. Beat egg yolks slightly. To plump raisins, in mixing bowl cover raisins with boiling water and let stand 5 minutes; drain. For filling, in mixing bowl combine the sugar and flour; stir in orange juice and beaten egg yolks. Stir chopped rhubarb and raisins into sugar mixture. Place pie shell on oven rack; pour rhubarb filling into the partially baked pastry shell. To prevent overbrowning, cover edge of pie with foil. Bake in 350° oven for 30 minutes. Remove foil; bake about 25 minutes more or till filling is nearly set. *(Pie appears soft in center but becomes firm after cooling.)*

Make Meringue for Pie using the 3 reserved egg whites. Spread meringue over hot filling; seal to edge. Bake in 350° oven for 12 to 15 minutes more or till meringue is golden. Cool before serving. Cover; chill to store.

Lemon-Raisin Pie

Pastry for Single-Crust Pie (see
  recipe, page 84)
1½ cups raisins
  Boiling water
6 eggs
1½ cups sugar
½ cup coarsely chopped walnuts
¼ cup lemon juice
¼ cup butter *or* margarine, melted
½ teaspoon ground cinnamon
½ teaspoon ground nutmeg
¼ teaspoon salt

Prepare and roll out pastry. Line a 9-inch pie plate. Trim to ½ inch beyond edge of pie plate. Flute edge high; do not prick. Bake in 450° oven for 5 minutes. Cool on rack.

To plump raisins, in mixing bowl cover raisins with boiling water and let stand 5 minutes; drain.

For filling, in mixing bowl slightly beat eggs with rotary beater or fork. Stir in sugar, nuts, lemon juice, butter or margarine, cinnamon, nutmeg, salt, and raisins; mix well. Place pie shell on oven rack; pour filling into the partially baked pastry shell. To prevent overbrowning, cover edge of pie with foil. Bake in 375° oven for 20 minutes. Remove foil; bake for 20 minutes more or till knife inserted off-center comes out clean. Cool on rack before serving. Cover; chill to store.

Mandarin-Banana Custard Pie

Graham Cracker Crust (see
  recipe, page 92)
2½ cups milk
1 4½-ounce package no-bake
  custard mix
1 8-ounce package cream cheese,
  cubed
¾ teaspoon finely shredded
  orange peel
1 large banana, sliced
⅔ cup orange juice
2 teaspoons cornstarch
1 11-ounce can mandarin orange
  sections, drained

Prepare the Graham Cracker Crust. Press crumb mixture onto bottom and sides of a 9-inch pie plate. Bake in 375° oven for 6 to 8 minutes or till browned. Cool.

For filling, in saucepan combine milk and custard mix. Stir in cubed cream cheese and orange peel. Cook till mixture is thickened and bubbly, stirring constantly. Remove from heat; beat with rotary beater at low speed till smooth. Cool 15 minutes. Arrange the banana slices in bottom of baked crumb crust. Carefully pour custard mixture over banana layer. Chill several hours or till set.

For sauce, in saucepan combine orange juice and cornstarch. Cook and stir till thickened and bubbly. Cool slightly; stir in orange sections. Serve sauce warm or chilled. To serve, spoon some sauce over pie and pass remaining.

Cottage Cheesecake Pie

Graham Cracker Crust (see
   recipe, page 92)
1½ cups cream-style cottage
   cheese, well-drained
 3 eggs
½ cup sugar
 2 tablespoons all-purpose flour
 1 tablespoon lemon juice
 1 teaspoon vanilla
 1 5⅓-ounce can (⅔ cup)
   evaporated milk
 1 21-ounce can blueberry pie
   filling, chilled

Prepare Graham Cracker Crust. Press crumb mixture onto bottom and sides of a 9-inch pie plate. Chill in refrigerator about 1 hour or till firm.

For filling, in mixer bowl beat drained cottage cheese with electric mixer or rotary beater about 5 minutes or till creamy and nearly smooth. Add eggs, sugar, flour, lemon juice, and vanilla; mix well to thoroughly combine. Stir in evaporated milk. Place chilled graham cracker pie shell on oven rack; pour filling into pie shell. Bake in 350° oven for 25 to 30 minutes or till knife inserted off-center comes out clean. Cool pie on rack; chill thoroughly before serving. Spread chilled blueberry pie filling atop pie before serving. Cover; chill to store.

Molasses-Mince Pie

Pastry for Single-Crust Pie
   (see recipe, page 84)
 2 beaten eggs
 1 5⅓-ounce can (⅔ cup)
   evaporated milk
½ cup sugar
 2 tablespoons light molasses
1½ cups prepared mincemeat
   Unsweetened whipped cream

Prepare and roll out pastry. Line a 9-inch pie plate. Trim to ½ inch beyond edge. Flute edge; do not prick. Bake in 450° oven for 5 minutes. Cool thoroughly on rack.

For filling, combine eggs, evaporated milk, sugar, and molasses; mix well. Stir in mincemeat. Place pie shell on oven rack; pour in filling. To prevent overbrowning, cover edge of pie with foil. Bake in 375° oven for 20 minutes. Remove foil; bake for 20 to 25 minutes more or till knife inserted off-center comes out clean. Cool. Garnish pie with unsweetened whipped cream. Cover; chill to store.

Miracle Custard Pie

 2 cups milk
 4 eggs
½ cup sugar
½ cup all-purpose flour
¼ cup butter *or* margarine, cut-up
 1 teaspoon vanilla
 1 cup flaked coconut
   Ground nutmeg

In blender container combine milk, eggs, sugar, flour, cut-up butter or margarine, vanilla, and ¼ teaspoon *salt*. Cover; blend about 10 seconds or till well-mixed *(do not overblend)*. Stir in coconut. Pour egg mixture into greased 9-inch pie plate. Sprinkle a little nutmeg atop filling. Bake in 350° oven about 40 minutes or till knife inserted off-center comes out clean. *(As pie bakes, it forms its own soft crust.)* Cool pie on rack; chill thoroughly before serving. Cover; chill to store.

Sour Cream-Plum Pie

Pastry for Single-Crust Pie
   (see recipe, page 84)
 1 30-ounce can purple plums,
   drained
 2 cups dairy sour cream
 2 slightly beaten egg yolks
½ cup sugar
 1 teaspoon vanilla

Prepare and roll out pastry. Line a 9-inch pie plate. Trim to ½ inch beyond edge. Flute edge; prick pastry. Bake in 450° oven for 10 to 12 minutes. Cool on rack.

Halve and pit plums; arrange skin-side-down in bottom of cooled pastry shell. Combine sour cream, egg yolks, sugar, and vanilla. Spread mixture over plums. To prevent overbrowning, cover edge of pie with foil. Bake in 350° oven for 45 minutes or till sour cream mixture is set. Cool; chill thoroughly before serving. Cover; chill to store.

Fresh Peach Custard Pie

**Pastry for Single-Crust Pie
(see recipe, page 84)**
3 cups sliced fresh *or* frozen
peaches
⅔ cup sugar
2 tablespoons all-purpose flour
¼ teaspoon salt
2 slightly beaten eggs
1 cup light cream *or* milk
Ground nutmeg

Prepare and roll out pastry. Line a 9-inch pie plate. Trim pastry to ½ inch beyond edge. Flute edge; do not prick. Bake in 450° oven for 5 minutes. Cool. Thaw peaches, if frozen; drain peaches. Thinly slice peaches.

For filling, place sliced peaches in bottom of partially baked pastry shell. In mixing bowl combine sugar, flour, and salt; stir in eggs. Stir in light cream or milk. Place pie shell on oven rack. Carefully pour filling over peaches. Sprinkle a little nutmeg atop. To prevent overbrowning, cover edge of pie with foil. Bake in 350° oven for 25 minutes. Remove foil; bake for 20 to 25 minutes more or till knife inserted off-center comes out clean. Cool on rack before serving. Cover; chill to store.

Apricot Custard Pie

**Pastry for Single-Crust Pie
(see recipe, page 84)**
1 cup snipped dried apricots
(4 ounces)
Water
¼ cup sugar
3 slightly beaten eggs
2 cups buttermilk
¾ cup sugar
Dash salt

Prepare and roll out pastry. Line a 9-inch pie plate. Trim to ½ inch beyond edge. Flute edge; do not prick. Bake in 450° oven for 5 minutes. Cool on rack.

For filling, in small saucepan cover snipped apricots with water 1 inch above the fruit. Cover; bring to boiling. Reduce heat and simmer for 15 to 20 minutes; drain well. Stir the ¼ cup sugar into drained apricots. Cool mixture slightly. In mixing bowl combine beaten eggs, buttermilk, the ¾ cup sugar, and salt; mix well. Spread apricot mixture evenly in bottom of the partially baked pastry shell. Place pie shell on oven rack. Carefully pour buttermilk filling over apricot layer.

To prevent overbrowning, cover edge of pie with foil. Bake in 350° oven for 20 minutes. Remove foil; bake for 25 to 30 minutes more or till nearly set. *(Pie appears soft in center but becomes firm after cooling.)* Cool pie thoroughly on rack before serving. Cover; chill to store.

Pear-Cheesecake Pie

**Graham Cracker Crust (see
recipe, page 92)**
1 8-ounce package cream cheese,
softened
2 eggs
1 cup dairy sour cream
½ teaspoon finely shredded lemon
peel
1 teaspoon lemon juice
½ cup sugar
1 tablespoon all-purpose flour
½ teaspoon salt
½ teaspoon ground nutmeg
1 16-ounce can pear halves,
well-drained and coarsely
chopped
Unsweetened whipped cream

Prepare Graham Cracker crust. Press crumb mixture firmly onto bottom and sides of a 9-inch pie plate. Chill about 1 hour or till firm.

For filling, in mixer bowl beat cream cheese with electric mixer or rotary beater till fluffy. Stir in eggs, sour cream, lemon peel, and lemon juice. Add sugar, flour, salt, and nutmeg; beat till smooth. Stir in chopped pears. Turn filling into chilled crumb crust. Bake in 375° oven for 30 minutes or just till filling is set. Cool on rack; chill thoroughly before serving. To serve, garnish pie with unsweetened whipped cream; sprinkle lightly with some additional graham cracker crumbs, if desired. Cover; chill to store.

Squash Pie

Pastry for Single-Crust Pie
   (see recipe, page 84)
 2 cups mashed cooked winter
   squash
½ cup sugar
 1 tablespoon butter *or* margarine,
   melted
 1 teaspoon ground cinnamon
½ teaspoon salt
¼ teaspoon ground ginger
¼ teaspoon ground nutmeg
1¾ cups milk
 2 slightly beaten eggs
 1 teaspoon vanilla
   Unsweetened whipped cream
   (optional)

Prepare and roll out pastry. Line a 9-inch pie plate. Trim pastry to ½ inch beyond edge of pie plate. Flute edge high; do not prick pastry. Bake in 450° oven for 5 minutes. Cool thoroughly on rack.

Using a sieve, drain mashed squash well to remove any excess liquid. For filling, in mixing bowl combine drained squash, sugar, melted butter or margarine, cinnamon, salt, ginger, and nutmeg. Stir in milk, beaten eggs, and vanilla. Place partially baked pie shell on oven rack; pour in filling. To prevent overbrowning, cover edge of pie with foil. Bake in 375° oven for 30 minutes. Remove foil; bake about 20 minutes more or till nearly set. *(Pie appears soft in center but becomes firm after cooling.)* Cool pie on rack before serving. Garnish with unsweetened whipped cream, if desired. Cover; chill to store.

Shoofly Pie

Pastry for Single-Crust Pie
   (see recipe, page 84)
1½ cups all-purpose flour
½ cup packed brown sugar
 6 tablespoons butter *or* margarine
½ cup light molasses
½ cup hot water
½ teaspoon baking soda

Prepare and roll out pastry. Line a 9-inch pie plate. Trim pastry to ½ inch beyond edge of pie plate. Flute edge; do not prick pastry. Bake in 450° oven for 5 minutes. Cool thoroughly on rack.

For filling, in mixing bowl stir together flour and brown sugar. Cut in butter or margarine till mixture resembles coarse crumbs. In another mixing bowl combine molasses, hot water, and baking soda. Pour ⅓ of the molasses mixture into bottom of partially baked pastry shell. Sprinkle ⅓ of the flour mixture atop molasses layer. Repeat layers, ending with flour mixture. To prevent overbrowning, cover edge of pie with foil. Bake in 375° oven for 15 minutes. Remove foil; bake for 15 to 20 minutes more or till filling is set. Cool pie on rack before serving. Cover; chill to store.

Lemon-Chess Pie

Pastry for Single-Crust Pie
   (see recipe, page 84)
 5 eggs
1½ cups sugar
 1 cup light cream *or* milk
¼ cup butter *or* margarine, melted
 1 teaspoon finely shredded
   lemon peel
 2 tablespoons lemon juice
 1 tablespoon all-purpose flour
 1 tablespoon yellow cornmeal
1½ teaspoons vanilla

Prepare and roll out pastry. Line a 9-inch pie plate. Trim pastry to ½ inch beyond edge of pie plate. Flute edge; do not prick pastry. Bake in 450° oven for 5 minutes. Cool on rack.

For filling, in medium mixing bowl beat eggs till well-blended. Stir in sugar, light cream or milk, melted butter or margarine, shredded lemon peel, lemon juice, flour, cornmeal, and vanilla. Mix well to combine thoroughly.

Place pie shell on oven rack. Pour filling into the partially baked pastry shell. To prevent overbrowning, cover edge of pie with foil. Bake in 350° oven for 20 minutes. Remove foil; bake for 20 to 25 minutes more or till knife inserted off-center comes out clean. Cool pie on rack before serving. Cover; chill to store.

4 Refreshing Refrigerated Pies

Try any of our glamorous refrigerated pies for a refreshing dessert that's bound to please every after-dinner appetite.

Strawberry Chiffon Pie
(see recipe, page 58)

Create a Refrigerated Pie

Strawberry Chiffon Pie (pictured on page 57)

**Pastry for Single-Crust Pie
(see recipe, page 84)**
2½ **cups fresh strawberries**
¼ **cup sugar**
1 **tablespoon lemon juice**
¼ **cup sugar**
1 **envelope unflavored gelatin**
¾ **cup water**
2 **egg whites**
¼ **cup sugar**
½ **cup whipping cream**

Prepare and roll out pastry. Line a 9-inch pie plate. Trim pastry to ½ inch beyond edge. Flute edge; prick pastry. Bake in a 450° oven for 10 to 12 minutes or till golden. Cool on rack.

1 Reserve a few strawberries for garnish; set aside. In large mixing bowl crush enough of the remaining strawberries to measure 1¼ cups crushed berries. Stir in ¼ cup sugar and the lemon juice; let berry mixture stand 30 minutes.

2 Meanwhile, in small saucepan stir together ¼ cup sugar and the gelatin. Stir in the water; heat and stir till sugar and gelatin dissolve. Cool. Stir the cooled gelatin mixture into the strawberry mixture. Chill to the consistency of corn syrup, stirring occasionally. Remove from refrigerator (gelatin mixture will continue to set).

3 Immediately begin beating egg whites till soft peaks form. **4-5** Gradually add ¼ cup sugar, beating till stiff peaks form. **6** When gelatin is the consistency of unbeaten egg whites (partially set), fold in stiff-beaten egg whites.

7 Beat whipping cream till soft peaks form. Fold whipped cream into strawberry mixture. Chill till mixture mounds when spooned. **8** Pile mixture into baked pastry shell. Chill pie 8 hours or till firm. Garnish with reserved strawberries. Serve with additional whipped cream, if desired.

1
Set aside a few of the prettiest strawberries for garnish. In a large mixing bowl crush enough of the remaining berries to measure 1¼ cups crushed berries. Use a potato masher to crush the berries. Stir in ¼ cup sugar and the lemon juice; let stand 30 minutes.

2
Stir together ¼ cup sugar and gelatin; stir in the water. Heat, stirring constantly, till sugar and gelatin dissolve. Cool. Stir cooled gelatin mixture into the strawberry mixture. Chill mixture to the consistency of corn syrup, stirring occasionally. Remove from refrigerator while beating egg whites to prevent excessive setting of gelatin mixture.

3
In mixer bowl beat egg whites at medium speed of electric mixer about 1 minute or till soft peaks form.

At this stage, the egg white foam turns white and the tips of the peaks bend over in soft curls when beaters are removed, as shown.

4

Gradually add ¼ cup sugar, about a tablespoon at a time, beating at high speed of electric mixer about 3 minutes or till mixture forms stiff peaks. Using a rubber spatula, guide egg whites toward beaters to thoroughly beat in the sugar.

The sugar helps to stabilize the foam, thus preventing it from separating.

5

When the egg white mixture forms stiff peaks, the foam becomes even whiter and forms glossy peaks that stand up straight when the beaters are removed, as shown. The egg white mixture now contains all of the air it is capable of holding, and the sugar granules are dissolved to prevent a grainy texture.

6

While beating egg whites, the gelatin mixture continues to set and should now be the consistency of unbeaten egg whites (partially set). Fold stiff-beaten egg whites into gelatin mixture. To fold, cut down through mixture with rubber spatula; scrape across bottom of bowl. Then bring spatula up and over mixture, close to surface, Repeat this circular down-up-and-over motion.

7

Beat whipping cream till soft peaks form. Peaks should mound slightly when beaters are removed, as shown.

Fold the whipped cream into the strawberry mixture (see step 6).

Chill till mixture mounds when dropped from a spoon (the mixture may mound without chilling).

8

Pile the strawberry mixture into the baked pastry shell. Use a rubber spatula or a wooden spoon to guide the mixture into the pastry shell.

Chill the pie for 8 hours or overnight till firm. Garnish with the reserved strawberries. Serve with additional whipped cream, if desired.

Pie-Making Tips

- Chiffon pies can be tricky, so it's important to fully understand the technique. For a smooth pie, the gelatin needs to be of the proper consistency.
- First chill the gelatin mixture to the consistency of corn syrup, stirring occasionally. Remove from refrigerator (gelatin mixture will continue to set). Beat the egg whites to stiff peaks. When the gelatin mixture is the consistency of unbeaten egg whites—slightly thicker than corn syrup, but still pourable—fold it into the stiff-beaten egg whites. Fold whipped cream into the mixture. To obtain a fluffy filling, chill the mixture till it mounds slightly when spooned.

Raspberry Chiffon Pie (pictured on page 4)

**Pastry for Single-Crust Pie
(see recipe, page 84)**
**1 10-ounce package frozen red
raspberries, thawed**
**1 3-ounce package raspberry-
flavored gelatin**
2 tablespoons sugar
2 tablespoons lemon juice
2 egg whites
¼ cup sugar
**1 cup whipping cream
Mint sprigs (optional)**

Prepare and roll out pastry. Line a 9-inch pie plate. Trim pastry to ½ inch beyond edge of pie plate. Flute edge; prick bottom and sides of pastry with tines of fork. Bake in 450° oven for 10 to 12 minutes or till golden. Cool thoroughly on wire rack.

Drain thawed red raspberries, reserving the syrup. Reserve 6 raspberries for garnish; set aside. Add enough water to the reserved raspberry syrup to measure 1½ cups liquid.

In a small saucepan combine raspberry gelatin and the 2 tablespoons sugar. Stir in the 1½ cups berry liquid and lemon juice. Heat mixture, stirring constantly, till sugar and gelatin dissolve. Cool.

Stir the cooled gelatin mixture into the drained raspberries. Chill gelatin mixture to the consistency of corn syrup, stirring occasionally.

Immediately beat egg whites till soft peaks form. Gradually add the ¼ cup sugar, beating till stiff peaks form. When gelatin is the consistency of unbeaten egg whites (partially set), fold in stiff-beaten egg whites. Whip cream till soft peaks form. Fold into gelatin mixture. Chill till mixture mounds when spooned.

Turn gelatin-whipped cream mixture into baked pastry shell. Chill several hours or overnight till set. Arrange the reserved raspberries around edge of pie. Trim with fresh mint sprigs, if desired. Cover; chill to store.

Layered Pumpkin Chiffon Pie

**Gingersnap-Graham Crust
(see recipe, page 92)**
⅓ cup granulated sugar
1 envelope unflavored gelatin
½ teaspoon salt
½ teaspoon ground cinnamon
½ teaspoon ground allspice
¼ teaspoon ground ginger
¼ teaspoon ground nutmeg
3 slightly beaten egg yolks
1 cup canned pumpkin
½ cup milk
3 egg whites
¼ cup granulated sugar
1 cup whipping cream
¼ cup sifted powdered sugar
½ teaspoon vanilla
¼ teaspoon ground cinnamon

Prepare Gingersnap-Graham Crust; press crumb mixture onto bottom and sides of a buttered 9-inch pie plate. Bake in 375° oven for 4 to 5 minutes or till browned. Cool.

In saucepan combine the ⅓ cup granulated sugar, gelatin, salt, the ½ teaspoon cinnamon, allspice, ginger, and nutmeg. Combine egg yolks, pumpkin, and milk; stir into gelatin mixture in saucepan. Cook and stir over medium heat till gelatin dissolves and mixture thickens slightly. Remove from heat. Chill gelatin mixture to the consistency of corn syrup, stirring occasionally.

Immediately beat egg whites till soft peaks form. Gradually add the ¼ cup granulated sugar, beating till stiff peaks form. When gelatin is consistency of unbeaten egg whites (partially set), fold in stiff-beaten egg whites. Pile *half* the egg white-gelatin mixture into baked crumb crust; set remainder aside.

Combine whipping cream, powdered sugar, vanilla, and the ¼ teaspoon cinnamon. Cover and refrigerate *half* the mixture. Whip remaining half till soft peaks form; spread over egg white-gelatin layer in crumb crust. Top with remaining gelatin mixture; chill several hours or overnight till set. To serve, whip reserved whipping cream mixture and pass with pie. Cover; chill to store.

Peanut Brittle Pie

Pastry for Single-Crust Pie
(see recipe, page 84)
⅔ cup packed brown sugar
1 envelope unflavored gelatin
Dash salt
⅓ cup water
2 slightly beaten egg yolks
2 tablespoons butter or margarine
½ cup milk
1 teaspoon vanilla
2 egg whites
2 tablespoons granulated sugar
½ cup crushed peanut brittle
½ cup whipping cream

Prepare and roll out pastry. Line 9-inch pie plate. Trim to ½ inch beyond edge. Flute edge; prick pastry. Bake in 450° oven for 10 to 12 minutes or till golden. Cool.

Combine brown sugar, gelatin, and salt. Stir in water and egg yolks. Cook and stir over medium heat till mixture thickens slightly. Remove from heat. Add butter, stirring till melted. Stir in milk and vanilla. Chill to the consistency of corn syrup, stirring occasionally.

Immediately beat egg whites till soft peaks form. Gradually add granulated sugar, beating till stiff peaks form. When gelatin is the consistency of unbeaten egg whites (partially set), fold in stiff-beaten egg whites and crushed peanut brittle. Whip cream till soft peaks form. Fold into gelatin mixture. Chill till mixture mounds when spooned. Turn mixture into baked pastry shell. Chill several hours or overnight till set. Cover and chill to store.

Buttermint Chiffon Pie

Chocolate Wafer Crust (see recipe, page 92)
1 envelope unflavored gelatin
1¼ cups milk
3 slightly beaten egg yolks
24 buttermints, coarsely crushed (½ cup)
3 egg whites
¼ cup sugar
½ cup whipping cream
Unsweetened whipped cream (optional)
Chocolate curls (optional)

Prepare Chocolate Wafer Crust. Press crumb mixture onto bottom and sides of a 9-inch pie plate. Chill.

Soften gelatin in milk. Stir in egg yolks. Cook and stir over low heat till slightly thickened. Cool; stir in mints. Chill to the consistency of corn syrup; stir occasionally.

Immediately beat egg whites till soft peaks form. Gradually add sugar, beating till stiff peaks form. When gelatin is the consistency of unbeaten egg whites (partially set), fold in stiff-beaten egg whites. Whip the ½ cup whipping cream till soft peaks form. Fold into gelatin mixture. Chill till mixture mounds when spooned. Turn into wafer crust. Chill several hours or overnight till set. Garnish with additional unsweetened whipped cream and chocolate curls, if desired. Cover; chill to store.

Fruit Cocktail Chiffon Pie

Pastry for Single-Crust Pie
(see recipe, page 84)
1 17-ounce can fruit cocktail
1 envelope unflavored gelatin
2 tablespoons sugar
3 slightly beaten egg yolks
Dash salt
1 6-ounce can frozen pineapple juice concentrate
3 egg whites
⅓ cup sugar

Prepare and roll out pastry. Line a 9-inch pie plate. Trim to ½ inch beyond edge. Flute edge; prick pastry. Bake in 450° oven for 10 to 12 minutes or till golden. Cool.

Drain fruit cocktail, reserving syrup. In a saucepan combine gelatin and 2 tablespoons sugar; add the reserved syrup, egg yolks, and salt. Cook and stir over low heat till mixture thickens slightly. Remove from heat. Stir in pineapple concentrate. Chill to the consistency of corn syrup, stirring occasionally.

Immediately beat egg whites till soft peaks form. Gradually add ⅓ cup sugar, beating till stiff peaks form. When gelatin is the consistency of unbeaten egg whites (partially set), fold in stiff-beaten egg whites and fruit cocktail. Chill till mixture mounds when spooned. Turn into baked pastry shell. Chill several hours or overnight till set. Cover and chill to store.

Lime Daiquiri Pie

Pastry for Single-Crust Pie
(see recipe, page 84)
⅔ cup sugar
1 envelope unflavored gelatin
¼ teaspoon salt
½ teaspoon finely shredded
    lime peel (set aside)
⅓ cup lime juice
⅓ cup water
3 slightly beaten egg yolks
6 to 8 drops green food coloring
    (optional)
¼ cup light rum
3 egg whites
⅓ cup sugar

Prepare and roll out pastry. Line a 9-inch pie plate. Trim to ½ inch beyond edge. Flute edge; prick pastry. Bake in 450° oven for 10 to 12 minutes or till golden. Cool.

Combine ⅔ cup sugar, gelatin, and salt. Stir in lime juice, water, and egg yolks. Cook and stir over low heat till mixture thickens slightly. Remove from heat. Stir in lime peel; tint with food coloring, if desired. Cool slightly; stir in rum. Chill to the consistency of corn syrup, stirring occasionally. Immediately beat egg whites till soft peaks form. Gradually add ⅓ cup sugar, beating to stiff peaks. When gelatin is the consistency of unbeaten egg whites (partially set), fold in stiff-beaten egg whites. Chill till mixture mounds when spooned. Turn into baked pastry shell. Chill several hours or till set. If desired, garnish with unsweetened whipped cream, lime slices, and mint sprigs. Cover and chill to store.

High Citrus Pie

Pastry for Single-Crust Pie
(see recipe, page 84)
⅔ cup sugar
1 envelope unflavored gelatin
¼ teaspoon salt
½ teaspoon finely shredded
    lemon peel (set aside)
½ cup lemon juice
1 teaspoon finely shredded
    orange peel (set aside)
¼ cup orange juice
¼ cup water
5 slightly beaten egg yolks
5 egg whites
⅓ cup sugar

Prepare and roll out pastry. Line a 9-inch pie plate. Trim to ½ inch beyond edge. Flute edge; prick pastry. Bake in 450° oven for 10 to 12 minutes or till golden. Cool.

In saucepan combine ⅔ cup sugar, gelatin, and salt. Stir in lemon juice, orange juice, water, and egg yolks. Cook and stir just till mixture thickens slightly. Remove from heat; stir in lemon and orange peels. Chill to the consistency of corn syrup, stirring occasionally.

Immediately beat egg whites till soft peaks form. Gradually add ⅓ cup sugar, beating to stiff peaks. When gelatin is the consistency of unbeaten egg whites (partially set), fold in stiff-beaten egg whites. Chill till mixture mounds when spooned. Turn into baked pastry shell. Chill several hours or overnight till set. If desired, garnish with orange slices and maraschino cherries. Cover and chill to store.

Lemon Chiffon Pie

Pastry for Single-Crust Pie
(see recipe, page 84)
½ cup sugar
1 envelope unflavored gelatin
½ teaspoon salt
⅔ cup water
1 teaspoon finely shredded
    lemon peel (set aside)
⅓ cup lemon juice
4 slightly beaten egg yolks
4 egg whites
½ cup sugar
½ cup whipping cream

Prepare and roll out pastry. Line a 9-inch pie plate. Trim to ½ inch beyond edge. Flute edge; prick pastry. Bake in 450° oven for 10 to 12 minutes or till golden. Cool.

Combine ½ cup sugar, gelatin, and salt. Stir in water, lemon juice, and egg yolks. Cook and stir over medium heat till mixture thickens slightly. Remove from heat; stir in lemon peel.

Chill gelatin mixture to the consistency of corn syrup, stirring occasionally. Immediately beat egg whites till soft peaks form. Gradually add ½ cup sugar, beating to stiff peaks. When gelatin is the consistency of unbeaten egg whites (partially set), fold in stiff-beaten egg whites. Whip cream till soft peaks form. Fold into gelatin mixture. Chill till mixture mounds when spooned. Turn into baked pastry shell. Chill several hours or overnight till set. Cover and chill to store.

Lime Daiquiri Pie, *High Citrus Pie,* and *Peach Parfait Pie* (see recipe, page 72)
are a trio of light, refreshing choices to top off summer meals—no matter what the occasion.

Black Bottom Pie

**Pastry for Single-Crust Pie
(see recipe, page 84)**
½ cup sugar
1 tablespoon cornstarch
2 cups milk
4 slightly beaten egg yolks
1 teaspoon vanilla
1 6-ounce package (1 cup)
semisweet chocolate
pieces
1 envelope unflavored gelatin
¼ cup cold water
½ teaspoon rum extract *or* 2
tablespoons light rum
4 egg whites
½ cup sugar
Pecan halves

Prepare and roll out pastry. Line a 9-inch pie plate. Trim to ½ inch beyond edge. Flute edge; prick pastry. Bake in 450° oven for 10 to 12 minutes or till golden. Cool.

In saucepan combine ½ cup sugar and cornstarch. Stir in milk and egg yolks. Cook and stir over medium heat till mixture thickens and coats a metal spoon. Remove from heat; stir in vanilla. Stir chocolate into *1 ¼ cups* of the thickened mixture till melted; pour into baked shell. Chill.

Meanwhile, soften gelatin in cold water. Stir into remaining *hot* thickened mixture till gelatin dissolves. Stir in rum extract or rum. Chill to the consistency of corn syrup, stirring occasionally. Immediately beat egg whites till soft peaks form. Gradually add ½ cup sugar, beating till stiff peaks form. When gelatin is the consistency of unbeaten egg whites (partially set), fold in stiff-beaten egg whites. Chill till mixture mounds when spooned. Spread over pie. Chill several hours or till set. Garnish with pecans. Cover and chill to store.

Fudge Chiffon Pie

**Pastry for Single-Crust Pie
(see recipe, page 84)**
1 envelope unflavored gelatin
¼ cup cold water
3 egg yolks
⅓ cup sugar
1 teaspoon vanilla
¼ teaspoon salt
2 squares (2 ounces)
unsweetened chocolate
½ cup water
3 egg whites
½ cup sugar

Prepare and roll out pastry. Line a 9-inch pie plate. Trim to ½ inch beyond edge. Flute edge; prick pastry. Bake in 450° oven for 10 to 12 minutes or till golden. Cool.

Soften gelatin in ¼ cup cold water. In small mixer bowl beat egg yolks on high speed of electric mixer about 5 minutes or till thick and lemon-colored. Gradually beat in ⅓ cup sugar; stir in vanilla and salt. In saucepan combine chocolate and ½ cup water. Cook and stir over low heat till chocolate melts. Add to gelatin; stir to dissolve gelatin. Gradually beat gelatin mixture into egg yolk mixture. Chill to the consistency of corn syrup, stirring occasionally. Immediately beat egg whites till soft peaks form. Gradually add ½ cup sugar, beating till stiff peaks form. When gelatin is the consistency of unbeaten egg whites (partially set), fold in stiff-beaten egg whites. Chill till mixture mounds when spooned. Turn into baked shell. Chill. Cover and chill to store.

Coffee-and-Cream Chiffon Pie

**Vanilla Wafer Crust
(see recipe, page 92)**
⅓ cup sugar
3 tablespoons instant coffee
crystals
1 envelope unflavored gelatin
¼ teaspoon salt
1½ cups milk
2 slightly beaten egg yolks
1 teaspoon vanilla
2 egg whites
¼ cup sugar
½ cup whipping cream

Prepare Vanilla Wafer Crust. Press mixture onto bottom and sides of 9-inch pie plate. Chill. In saucepan mix ⅓ cup sugar, coffee crystals, gelatin, and salt. Stir in milk and egg yolks. Cook and stir till slightly thickened; remove from heat. Stir in vanilla; pour into large bowl. Chill to the consistency of corn syrup, stirring occasionally.

Immediately beat egg whites till soft peaks form. Add ¼ cup sugar, beating till stiff peaks form. When gelatin is the consistency of unbeaten egg whites (partially set), fold in stiff-beaten egg whites. Whip cream till soft peaks form; fold into gelatin mixture. Chill till mixture mounds when spooned. Turn into crust. Chill several hours or till set. Cover; chill to store.

Apple Swirl Chiffon Pie

Pastry for Single-Crust Pie
  (see recipe, page 84)
¼ **cup sugar**
1 **envelope unflavored gelatin**
¼ **teaspoon salt**
1⅓ **cups milk**
1 **cup tiny marshmallows**
2 **slightly beaten egg yolks**
½ **teaspoon finely shredded**
  lemon peel
2 **teaspoons lemon juice**
2 **egg whites**
2 **tablespoons sugar**
½ **cup whipping cream**
1 **cup apple butter**

Prepare and roll out pastry. Line a 9-inch pie plate. Trim pastry to ½ inch beyond edge of pie plate. Flute edge; prick bottom and sides of pastry with tines of a fork. Bake in 450° oven for 10 to 12 minutes or till golden. Cool thoroughly on wire rack.

In saucepan combine ¼ cup sugar, unflavored gelatin, and salt. Stir in milk; add marshmallows. Cook, stirring constantly, till gelatin dissolves and marshmallows melt. Stir about *half* the hot mixture into the beaten egg yolks; return to remaining hot mixture in saucepan. Cook and stir for 2 minutes. Cool gelatin mixture slightly; stir in finely shredded lemon peel and lemon juice. Turn into a large bowl. Chill gelatin mixture to the consistency of corn syrup, stirring occasionally.

Immediately beat egg whites till soft peaks form. Gradually add 2 tablespoons sugar, beating till stiff peaks form. When gelatin is the consistency of unbeaten egg whites (partially set), fold in stiff-beaten egg whites. Whip cream till soft peaks form; fold into gelatin-egg white mixture. Chill till mixture mounds when spooned. Spoon apple butter over gelatin mixture; fold in just till marbled. Turn into baked pastry shell. Chill several hours or overnight till set. Cover; chill to store.

Peach Chiffon Pie

Pastry for Single-Crust Pie
  (see recipe, page 84)
1 **29-ounce can peach halves**
¼ **cup sugar**
1 **envelope unflavored gelatin**
¼ **teaspoon salt**
½ **teaspoon finely shredded**
  lemon peel
2 **tablespoons lemon juice**
3 **slightly beaten egg yolks**
3 **egg whites**
⅓ **cup sugar**
  Unsweetened whipped cream
  (optional)

Prepare and roll out pastry. Line a 9-inch pie plate. Trim pastry to ½ inch beyond edge of pie plate. Flute edge; prick bottom and sides of pastry with tines of a fork. Bake in 450° oven for 10 to 12 minutes or till golden. Cool thoroughly on wire rack.

Drain canned peach halves, reserving ½ cup peach syrup and 1 peach half. Place the remaining peach halves in a blender container. Cover and blend just till peaches are pureed; set aside.

In saucepan combine ¼ cup sugar, unflavored gelatin, and salt. Stir in the ½ cup reserved syrup, finely shredded lemon peel, lemon juice, and egg yolks. Cook, stirring constantly, till gelatin is dissolved and mixture is slightly thickened and bubbly. Add the pureed peaches. Chill gelatin mixture to the consistency of corn syrup, stirring occasionally.

Immediately beat egg whites till soft peaks form. Gradually add ⅓ cup sugar, beating till stiff peaks form. When gelatin is the consistency of unbeaten egg whites (partially set), fold in stiff-beaten egg whites. Chill till mixture mounds when spooned. Turn into baked pastry shell. Chill several hours or overnight till set.

To serve, slice the reserved peach half. Garnish chilled pie with the peach slices. Top with dollops of unsweetened whipped cream, if desired. Cover; chill to store.

Pumpkin Chiffon Tarts

Pastry for Double-Crust Pie
(see recipe, page 87)
¾ cup packed brown sugar
1 envelope unflavored gelatin
1 teaspoon ground cinnamon
½ teaspoon salt
¼ teaspoon ground nutmeg
¼ teaspoon ground ginger
¾ cup milk
3 slightly beaten egg yolks
1¼ cups canned pumpkin
3 egg whites
¼ cup granulated sugar

Prepare pastry; divide in half. Roll *half* the pastry at a time to ⅛-inch thickness. Cut *each half* into five 4½-inch circles. Fit over inverted muffin pans, pinching pleats at intervals to fit around pans; prick pastry. Bake in 450° oven for 7 to 10 minutes or till golden. Cool.

In saucepan combine brown sugar, gelatin, cinnamon, salt, nutmeg, and ginger. Stir in milk and egg yolks. Cook and stir till slightly thickened. Remove from heat; stir in pumpkin. Chill to the consistency of corn syrup, stirring occasionally. Immediately beat egg whites till soft peaks form. Gradually add granulated sugar, beating till stiff peaks form. When gelatin is the consistency of unbeaten egg whites (partially set), fold in stiff-beaten egg whites. Chill till mixture mounds when spooned. Turn into baked tart shells. Chill several hours or overnight till set. Cover; chill to store. Makes 10 tarts.

Maple-Nut Chiffon Pie

Pastry for Single-Crust Pie
(see recipe, page 84)
1 envelope unflavored gelatin
¼ cup cold water
¾ cup milk
½ cup maple-flavored syrup
⅛ teaspoon salt
2 beaten egg yolks
1 teaspoon vanilla
2 egg whites
¾ cup whipping cream
⅓ cup chopped walnuts

Prepare and roll out pastry. Line a 9-inch pie plate. Trim to ½ inch beyond edge. Flute edge; prick pastry. Bake in 450° oven for 10 to 12 minutes or till golden. Cool.

Soften gelatin in cold water. Stir in milk, maple syrup, and salt. Heat till gelatin is dissolved. Stir about *half* the hot mixture into egg yolks; return to remaining hot mixture. Cook and stir 1 to 2 minutes more or till slightly thickened. Stir in vanilla. Chill to the consistency of corn syrup, stirring occasionally.

Immediately beat egg whites till stiff peaks form. When gelatin is the consistency of unbeaten egg whites (partially set), fold in stiff-beaten egg whites. Whip cream just till soft peaks form. Fold whipped cream and nuts into gelatin mixture. Chill till mixture mounds when spooned. Turn into baked pastry shell. Chill several hours or overnight till set. Cover and chill to store.

Blueberry Yogurt Chiffon Pie

Graham Cracker Crust
(see recipe, page 92)
¼ cup sugar
1 envelope unflavored gelatin
½ teaspoon salt
¼ cup water
2 slightly beaten egg yolks
1 cup cream-style cottage cheese
1 8-ounce carton (1 cup)
blueberry yogurt
2 egg whites
¼ cup sugar
Unsweetened whipped cream
(optional)

Prepare Graham-Cracker Crust. Press crumb mixture onto bottom and sides of a 9-inch pie plate. Chill. In saucepan combine ¼ cup sugar, gelatin, and salt; stir in water and egg yolks. Cook and stir till the mixture is slightly thickened; cool.

Sieve cottage cheese; stir in gelatin mixture. Add yogurt; beat till blended. Immediately beat egg whites till soft peaks form. Gradually add ¼ cup sugar, beating till stiff peaks form. Fold stiff-beaten egg whites into the gelatin mixture. Chill till mixture mounds when spooned. Turn into chilled crumb crust. Chill several hours or overnight till set. Garnish with unsweetened whipped cream, if desired. Chill and cover to store.

A baked meringue crust, hidden under a delicious fresh strawberry filling, and a fluffy whipped cream topper make a spectacular dessert combination in *Upside-Down Berry Pie*.

Upside-Down Berry Pie

**Pastry for Single-Crust Pie
(see recipe, page 84)**
2 **egg whites**
½ **teaspoon vanilla**
¼ **teaspoon cream of tartar**
¼ **cup sugar**
3 **cups fresh strawberries**
½ **cup sugar**
3 **tablespoons cornstarch**
1 **cup whipping cream**
Sliced strawberries

Prepare and roll out pastry. Line a 9-inch pie plate. Trim to ½ inch beyond edge. Flute edge; prick pastry. Bake in 450° oven for 10 to 12 minutes. Cool. For meringue, beat whites, vanilla, and cream of tartar till soft peaks form. Gradually add ¼ cup sugar; beat till stiff peaks form. Spread on bottom and sides of pastry. Bake in 350° oven 12 minutes; cool. Mash berries; add water to measure 2 cups. Combine ½ cup sugar and cornstarch; add mashed berries. Cook and stir till bubbly. Cook and stir 2 minutes more. Cool; spread over meringue. Chill. Whip cream; spread over pie. Top with sliced strawberries. Cover; chill to store.

French Silk Pie

Pastry for Single-Crust Pie (see recipe, page 84)
1 **cup sugar**
¾ **cup butter (*not* margarine)***
3 **squares (3 ounces) unsweetened chocolate, melted and cooled**
1½ **teaspoons vanilla**
3 **eggs**
  Unsweetened whipped cream (optional)
  Chocolate curls (optional)

Prepare and roll out pastry. Line a 9-inch pie plate. Trim pastry to ½ inch beyond edge of pie plate. Flute edge; prick bottom and sides of pastry with tines of a fork. Bake in 450° oven for 10 to 12 minutes or till golden. Cool on wire rack.

In small mixer bowl cream sugar and butter about 4 minutes or till light. Blend in cooled chocolate and vanilla. Add eggs, one at a time, beating on medium speed of electric mixer for 2 minutes after each addition, scraping sides of bowl constantly. Turn into baked pastry shell. Chill several hours or overnight till set. Garnish with whipped cream and chocolate curls, if desired. Cover and chill to store.

Note: Some brands of margarine produce a nonfluffy, sticky filling when used in this pie. The results were so unsatisfactory that we recommend using only butter.

Caramel-Pecan Pie

Graham Cracker Crust (see recipe, page 92)
28 **vanilla caramels (8 ounces)**
1¼ **cups milk**
1 **envelope unflavored gelatin**
¼ **cup cold water**
1 **teaspoon vanilla**
⅛ **teaspoon salt**
1 **cup whipping cream**
½ **cup chopped pecans**

Prepare Graham Cracker Crust. Press crumb mixture onto bottom and sides of a 9-inch pie plate. Chill.

In heavy saucepan heat vanilla caramels and milk over low heat for 20 to 30 minutes or till caramels are melted, stirring frequently. Meanwhile, soften unflavored gelatin in cold water. Add softened gelatin to caramel mixture; stir till gelatin is dissolved. Stir in vanilla and salt. Chill gelatin mixture to the consistency of corn syrup, stirring occasionally.*

Immediately whip cream till soft peaks form. When gelatin is the consistency of unbeaten egg whites (partially set), fold in whipped cream. Fold in nuts. Chill till mixture mounds when spooned. Turn into crumb crust. Chill several hours or overnight till set. Cover; chill to store.

Note: Watch gelatin mixture closely; caramels make the mixture set up very quickly.

Strawberry Yogurt Pie

Graham Cracker Crust (see recipe, page 92)
1 **3-ounce package strawberry-flavored gelatin**
1¼ **cups boiling water**
1 **8-ounce carton (1 cup) strawberry yogurt**
¼ **cup honey**
2½ **cups fresh strawberries**
  Unsweetened whipped cream

Prepare Graham Cracker Crust. Press crumb mixture onto bottom and sides of a 9-inch pie plate. Chill.

In mixing bowl combine strawberry-flavored gelatin and boiling water; stir till strawberry gelatin is dissolved. Beat in the strawberry yogurt and honey. Chill gelatin mixture to the consistency of unbeaten egg whites (partially set). Meanwhile, reserve a few whole strawberries for garnish. Slice the remaining strawberries.

Beat gelatin mixture with electric mixer for 1 to 2 minutes or till light and fluffy. Fold sliced strawberries into gelatin mixture. Chill till mixture mounds when spooned. Turn into crumb crust. Cover; chill several hours or overnight till set. Garnish with whipped cream and the reserved berries. Cover; chill to store.

Pineapple Fluff Pie

Coconut Crust
(see recipe, page 93)
1   3¼- or 3½-ounce package
    regular vanilla tapioca pudding
    mix
1   3-ounce package
    lemon-flavored gelatin
1¼ cups milk
½   of a 6-ounce can (⅓ cup) frozen
    pineapple juice concentrate
1   2-ounce envelope dessert
    topping mix
1   8¼-ounce can crushed
    pineapple, well-drained

Prepare Coconut Crust. Press mixture onto bottom and sides of a buttered 9-inch pie plate. Bake in 325° oven about 20 minutes or till golden. Cool on wire rack.

In saucepan combine pudding mix and gelatin. Stir in milk. Cook and stir till thickened and bubbly (mixture may appear curdled during cooking). Remove from heat. Stir in pineapple juice concentrate. Chill mixture to the consistency of unbeaten egg whites (partially set), stirring occasionally.

Prepare dessert topping mix according to package directions. Fold dessert topping into gelatin mixture. Fold in well-drained crushed pineapple. Chill till mixture mounds when spooned. Turn into coconut crust; chill several hours or overnight till set. Cover; chill to store.

Peach-Berry Pie

Vanilla Wafer Crust
(see recipe, page 92)
1½ cups chopped fresh peaches
½   cup fresh *or* frozen raspberries
½   cup sugar
1   3-ounce package
    lemon-flavored gelatin
1   cup boiling water
    Few drops almond extract
    Dash salt
1   cup whipping cream
    Fresh mint sprigs (optional)

Prepare Vanilla Wafer Crust. Press crumb mixture onto bottom and sides of a 9-inch pie plate. Chill. In bowl combine fresh peaches and fresh or frozen raspberries; sprinkle with sugar. Let fruit mixture stand about 30 minutes. Drain fruit, reserving juices. Add enough water to juices to measure ⅔ cup.

Meanwhile, in another bowl dissolve lemon gelatin in boiling water; cool. Stir in the reserved ⅔ cup juices, almond extract, and salt. Chill gelatin mixture to the consistency of corn syrup, stirring occasionally.

Whip cream till soft peaks form. When gelatin is the consistency of unbeaten egg whites (partially set), fold in whipped cream. Fold in drained fruit. Chill till mixture mounds when spooned. Turn into chilled wafer crumb crust. Chill pie several hours or overnight till set. Garnish with fresh mint sprigs, if desired. Cover, chill to store.

Cheesecake Fruit Pie

Gingersnap-Graham Crust
(see recipe, page 92)
2   cups tiny marshmallows *or* 20
    large marshmallows
2   tablespoons milk
1   cup dairy sour cream
1   3-ounce package cream cheese,
    softened
1   teaspoon vanilla
    Dash salt
1   17-ounce can fruit cocktail,
    drained

Prepare Gingersnap-Graham Crust. Press crumb mixture onto bottom and sides of a buttered 9-inch pie plate. Bake in 375° oven for 4 to 5 minutes or till browned. Cool.

In heavy saucepan heat marshmallows and milk over low heat till marshmallows are melted, stirring frequently. Cool about 10 minutes. In mixer bowl beat sour cream, softened cream cheese, vanilla, and salt with electric mixer till smooth. Stir in marshmallow mixture and drained fruit cocktail. Turn into baked crumb crust. Chill several hours or overnight till set. Cover; chill to store.

Combine pudding mix, frosting mix, chocolate, bananas, and rum flavoring to make
Banana-Rum Pie. You'll find it makes an impressive ending for a luncheon or dinner party.

Banana-Rum Pie

Pecan Pastry
(see recipe, page 93)
1 3- or 3⅛-ounce package *regular*
vanilla pudding mix
1 envelope unflavored gelatin
2¼ cups milk
1 package fluffy white frosting mix
(for 2-layer cake)
1½ teaspoons rum flavoring
Dash salt
Dash ground nutmeg
3 small bananas
½ square (½ ounce) semisweet
chocolate
1 teaspoon butter *or* margarine

Prepare and roll out pastry. Line a 9-inch pie plate. Trim pastry to ½ inch beyond edge of pie plate. Flute edge; prick bottom and sides of pastry with tines of a fork. Bake in 450° oven for 10 to 12 minutes or till golden. Cool thoroughly on wire rack.

In saucepan combine pudding mix and gelatin. Cook according to *pudding* package directions *except* use the 2¼ cups milk. Remove from heat; pour into a bowl. Cover surface with clear plastic wrap or waxed paper.

Prepare frosting mix according to package directions. Stir in rum flavoring, salt, and nutmeg. Fold hot gelatin mixture into frosting mixture. Slice 1 banana into baked pastry shell; cover with *half* gelatin-frosting mixture. Repeat with second banana and remaining gelatin-frosting mixture. Chill several hours or overnight till set.

Just before serving, diagonally slice the remaining banana and arrange in center of pie. In saucepan melt chocolate and butter; drizzle over banana slices. Cover; chill to store.

Lime Parfait Pie

Pastry for Single-Crust Pie
(see recipe, page 84)
1 3-ounce package
lime-flavored gelatin
½ cup boiling water
¾ teaspoon finely shredded
lime peel
¼ cup lime juice
1 pint vanilla ice cream
1 cup whipping cream
Unsweetened whipped cream
(optional)
Maraschino cherries (optional)

Prepare and roll out pastry. Line a 9-inch pie plate. Trim to ½ inch beyond edge of pie plate. Flute edge and prick bottom and sides of pastry with tines of fork. Bake in 450° oven for 10 to 12 minutes or till golden. Cool on wire rack.

In large bowl dissolve gelatin in boiling water. Stir in lime peel and lime juice. Add ice cream by spoonfuls, stirring till melted. Chill to the consistency of unbeaten egg whites (partially set). Whip the 1 cup whipping cream; fold into lime mixture. Chill till mixture mounds when spooned. Turn into baked shell. Chill several hours or overnight till set. Top with whipped cream and maraschino cherries, if desired. Cover; chill to store.

Pineapple Parfait Pie

Pastry for Single-Crust Pie
(see recipe, page 84)
1 8¼-ounce can crushed
pineapple
1 3-ounce package
lemon-flavored gelatin
1 pint pineapple *or* lemon sherbet
Unsweetened whipped cream

Prepare and roll out pastry. Line a 9-inch pie plate. Trim pastry to ½ inch beyond edge of pie plate. Flute edge and prick bottom and sides of pastry with tines of a fork. Bake in 450° oven for 10 to 12 minutes or till golden. Cool on rack.

Drain pineapple, reserving syrup. Add enough water to syrup to measure 1 cup liquid. In saucepan heat the 1 cup liquid to boiling; remove from heat. Add gelatin; stir till gelatin is dissolved. Add pineapple or lemon sherbet by spoonfuls, stirring till melted. Chill till mixture mounds when spooned. Fold in crushed pineapple. Turn mixture into baked pastry shell. Chill several hours or overnight till set. Garnish with whipped cream. Cover; chill to store.

Peach Parfait Pie (pictured on page 63)

Gingersnap-Graham Crust
(see recipe, page 92)
3½ cups peeled, sliced fresh
peaches*
¼ cup sugar*
1 3-ounce package
lemon-flavored gelatin
1 pint vanilla ice cream
Unsweetened whipped cream
Ground nutmeg

Prepare Gingersnap Crust. Press crumb mixture onto bottom and sides of a buttered 9-inch pie plate. Bake in 375° oven for 4 to 5 minutes or till browned. Cool on rack.

In mixing bowl combine peaches and sugar; toss gently to coat. Let the peaches stand about 15 minutes after mixing with sugar. Drain peaches, reserving the syrup and 10 peach slices. Add enough water to the reserved syrup to measure 1 cup liquid. Heat fruit liquid to boiling; remove from heat. Add gelatin; stir till gelatin is dissolved. Pour gelatin mixture into large mixing bowl. Add ice cream by spoonfuls, stirring till melted. Chill till mixture mounds when spooned. Fold in sliced peaches. Turn peach mixture into baked crust. Chill pie several hours or overnight till set. Arrange the reserved peach slices spoke-fashion atop pie. Garnish with whipped cream and sprinkle with nutmeg. Cover; chill to store.

*Note: You may substitute one 29-ounce can peach slices for the fresh peaches *and* omit the ¼ cup sugar. Drain canned peaches, reserving the syrup, and set aside 10 peach slices for garnish.

Cherry-Burgundy Pie

Pastry for Single Crust Pie
(see recipe, page 84)
1 16-ounce can pitted dark
sweet cherries
1 3-ounce package
cherry-flavored gelatin
1 pint vanilla ice cream
3 tablespoons red burgundy
1 teaspoon lemon juice
Unsweetened whipped cream

Prepare and roll out pastry. Line 9-inch pie plate. Trim to ½ inch beyond edge of pie plate. Flute edge; prick pastry. Bake in 450° oven 10 to 12 minutes. Cool.

Drain cherries, reserving syrup. Quarter cherries; set aside. Add enough water to syrup to measure 1 cup liquid.

In saucepan heat the 1 cup liquid till boiling; remove from heat. Add gelatin; stir till gelatin is dissolved. Pour gelatin mixture into large mixing bowl. Add ice cream by spoonfuls, stirring till melted. Stir in burgundy and lemon juice. Chill till mixture mounds when spooned. Fold cherries into ice cream mixture. Chill again, if necessary, till mixture mounds. Turn into baked shell. Chill several hours or overnight till set. Garnish with whipped cream. Cover; chill to store.

Cranberry Parfait Pie

Pastry for Single-Crust Pie
(see recipe, page 84)
¾ cup cranberry juice cocktail
1 3-ounce package
lemon-flavored gelatin
1 16-ounce can whole cranberry
sauce
1 teaspoon finely shredded
lemon peel
2 tablespoons lemon juice
1 pint vanilla ice cream
Sweetened whipped cream

Prepare and roll out pastry. Line a 9-inch pie plate. Trim pastry to ½ inch beyond edge of pie plate. Flute edge; prick bottom and sides of pastry. Bake in 450° oven for 10 to 12 minutes or till golden. Cool on wire rack.

In saucepan heat cranberry juice cocktail to boiling; remove from heat. Add gelatin; stir till gelatin is dissolved. Pour gelatin mixture into large mixing bowl. Stir in cranberry sauce, lemon peel, and juice. Add ice cream by spoonfuls, stirring till melted. Chill till mixture mounds when spooned. Turn into baked shell. Chill pie several hours or overnight. Garnish with whipped cream. Cover; chill to store.

5 Never-Better Ice Cream Pies

Invite ice cream fanciers over for dessert and serve them their favorite flavors in a tantalizing frozen pie. This section is full of interesting recipes to impress your guests.

Fudge Ribbon Pie
(see recipe, page 74)

Create an Ice Cream Pie

Fudge Ribbon Pie (pictured on page 73)

Pastry for Single-Crust Pie (see recipe, page 84)
1   5⅓-ounce can (⅔ cup) evaporated milk
2   squares (2 ounces) unsweetened chocolate
1   cup sugar
2   tablespoons butter *or* margarine
1   teaspoon vanilla
1   quart peppermint ice cream
3   egg whites
½   teaspoon vanilla
¼   teaspoon cream of tartar
⅓   cup sugar
¼   cup crushed peppermint candy

Prepare and roll out pastry. Line a 9-inch pie plate. Trim pastry to ½ inch beyond edge. Flute edge; prick pastry. Bake in 450° oven for 10 to 12 minutes. Cool.

1 Combine evaporated milk and chocolate. Cook and stir over low heat till chocolate is melted. **2** Stir in the 1 cup sugar and the butter or margarine. Cook over medium heat for 5 to 8 minutes more or till thickened, stirring occasionally. Stir in the 1 teaspoon vanilla. Cool.

3 In mixing bowl soften ice cream using wooden spoon to stir and press against side of bowl. Soften till just pliable. **4** Spoon *half* the ice cream into baked pastry shell. Return remaining ice cream to freezer. Cover with *half* the cooled chocolate sauce; freeze. Let remaining chocolate sauce stand at room temperature. Repeat layers with remaining ice cream and sauce, softening ice cream to spread, if necessary. Cover; freeze till firm.

5 Prepare meringue by beating egg whites, ½ teaspoon vanilla, and cream of tartar till soft peaks form. **6-7** Gradually add ⅓ cup sugar, beating to stiff peaks. **8** Fold *3 tablespoons* of the crushed candy into meringue.

Remove pie from freezer. Spread meringue over chocolate layer, carefully sealing to edge of pastry. Swirl the meringue in a circular motion to make decorative peaks. Place on a baking sheet. Bake in 475° oven for 3 to 5 minutes or till meringue is golden. Sprinkle with remaining 1 tablespoon crushed candy. Serve immediately.

1
For chocolate sauce, in a small saucepan combine the evaporated milk and chocolate squares. Cook milk and chocolate over low heat, stirring with a wooden spoon, about 15 minutes or till chocolate is melted and thoroughly blended with the milk.

2
Stir the 1 cup sugar and the butter or margarine into blended milk-chocolate mixture. Cook mixture over medium heat for 5 to 8 minutes more or till chocolate mixture is thickened and sugar is dissolved, stirring occasionally with a wooden spoon. Stir in the 1 teaspoon vanilla. Allow the chocolate sauce to cool.

3
In a medium mixing bowl soften peppermint ice cream using a wooden spoon to stir and press against side of the bowl. Soften ice cream till just pliable. For easier softening, turn bowl while pressing. If the ice cream begins to melt, return bowl to freezer till ice cream becomes firm.

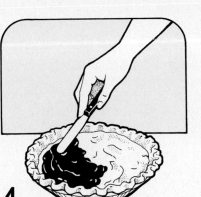

4

Spoon half of the softened ice cream into baked pastry shell. Return remaining ice cream to freezer. Spread half cooled chocolate sauce over ice cream layer to evenly cover. Freeze till firm. Let remaining sauce stand at room temperature. Repeat layers with remaining ice cream and sauce, softening ice cream to spread, if necessary. Cover; freeze till firm.

5

For meringue, in mixer bowl beat egg whites with the ½ teaspoon vanilla and cream of tartar at medium speed of electric mixer for about 1 minute or till soft peaks form.

At this stage, the egg white foam turns white and the tips of the peaks bend over in soft curls when beaters are removed, as shown.

6

Gradually add ⅓ cup sugar, about a tablespoon at a time, beating at high speed of electric mixer about 3 minutes or till mixture forms stiff peaks. Using a rubber spatula, guide egg whites toward beaters to thoroughly beat in the sugar.

The sugar helps to stabilize the foam, thus preventing it from separating.

7

When the egg white mixture forms stiff peaks, the foam becomes even whiter and forms glossy peaks that stand up straight when the beaters are removed, as shown. The egg white mixture now contains all of the air it is capable of holding, and the sugar granules are dissolved to prevent a grainy texture.

8

Fold 3 tablespoons of the crushed candy into meringue. Remove pie from freezer. Spread the meringue over chocolate layer, carefully sealing to edge of pastry. Swirl meringue to make decorative peaks. Place pie plate on baking sheet. Bake in 475° oven for 3 to 5 minutes or till meringue is golden. Sprinkle with remaining 1 tablespoon candy. Serve immediately.

Pie-Making Tips

● Frozen ice cream pies taste and serve better if they're removed from the freezer and allowed to soften for 10 to 15 minutes before serving. However, "baked alaska"-type pies should be served immediately after baking.

● Dip a knife in water before cutting a meringue-topped pie to prevent sticking (no need to dry knife). Repeat whenever meringue sticks.

● For a non-stick crumb crust, wrap a hot, wet towel under the bottom and around the sides of the pie plate just before serving the pie. Hold the towel against the plate for a few minutes; this loosens the crust so it will slip out easily.

Sundae Alaska Pie

Pastry for Single-Crust Pie
  (see recipe, page 84)
1 **pint strawberry ice cream**
½ **cup strawberry topping**
1 **pint lemon sherbet**
3 **egg whites**
½ **teaspoon vanilla**
¼ **teaspoon cream of tartar**
⅓ **cup sugar**

Prepare and roll out pastry. Line a 9-inch pie plate. Trim pastry to ½ inch beyond edge of pie plate. Flute edge; prick pastry with tines of a fork. Bake in 450° oven for 10 to 12 minutes or till pastry is golden. Cool thoroughly on rack.

In mixing bowl soften strawberry ice cream using a wooden spoon to stir and press against side of bowl. Soften till just pliable. Using a metal spatula, spread the softened ice cream in baked pastry shell. Immediately spread strawberry topping over ice cream layer in pastry shell. Freeze till firm.

In mixing bowl soften lemon sherbet using a wooden spoon to stir and press against side of bowl. Soften till just pliable. Spread the softened sherbet over the frozen strawberry topping layer. Return pie to freezer and freeze several hours or overnight till firm.

In mixer bowl prepare meringue by beating egg whites, vanilla, and cream of tartar till soft peaks form. Gradually add sugar, beating to stiff peaks. Spread meringue over frozen sherbet layer, carefully sealing to edge of pastry. Swirl the meringue in a circular motion to make decorative peaks.

Place the pie plate on a baking sheet. Bake in 475° oven for 3 to 5 minutes or till meringue is golden. Slice pie and serve immediately.

Lemon Alaska Pie

Pastry for Single-Crust Pie
  (see recipe, page 84)
1 **cup sugar**
6 **tablespoons butter *or* margarine**
⅓ **cup lemon juice**
  Dash salt
3 **egg yolks**
1 **egg**
1 **pint vanilla ice cream**
3 **egg whites**
½ **teaspoon vanilla**
¼ **teaspoon cream of tartar**
⅓ **cup sugar**
1 **teaspoon finely shredded**
  lemon peel

Prepare and roll out pastry. Line a 9-inch pie plate. Trim pastry to ½-inch beyond edge of pie plate. Flute edge; prick pastry. Bake in 450° oven for 10 to 12 minutes or till golden. Cool thoroughly on rack.

In saucepan combine 1 cup sugar, butter or margarine, lemon juice, and salt. Beat egg yolks and egg together slightly; stir into lemon mixture. Cook and stir over low heat till mixture is bubbly. Cover and chill.

In mixing bowl soften vanilla ice cream using a wooden spoon to stir and press against side of bowl. Soften till just pliable. Using a metal spatula, spread the softened ice cream in baked pastry shell. Top with chilled lemon mixture. Freeze several hours or overnight till firm.

In mixer bowl prepare meringue by beating egg whites, vanilla, and cream of tartar till soft peaks form. Gradually add ⅓ cup sugar, beating to stiff peaks. Fold in the shredded lemon peel.

Spread meringue over frozen lemon layer, carefully sealing to edge of pastry. Swirl the meringue in a circular motion to make decorative peaks. Place pie plate on a baking sheet. Bake in 475° oven for 3 to 5 minutes or till the meringue is golden. Slice pie and serve immediately.

Mincemeat Alaska Pie (pictured on page 4)

**Pastry for Single-Crust Pie
 (see recipe, page 84)**
1 **pint vanilla ice cream**
3 **egg whites**
½ **teaspoon vanilla**
¼ **teaspoon cream of tartar**
⅓ **cup sugar**
2½ **cups prepared mincemeat**
2 **tablespoons dry sherry**

Prepare and roll out pastry. Line a 9-inch pie plate. Trim to ½ inch beyond edge. Flute edge; prick pastry. Bake in 450° oven for 10 to 12 minutes or till golden. Cool.

In mixing bowl soften ice cream using a wooden spoon to stir and press against side of bowl. Soften till just pliable. Spread ice cream in baked pastry shell. Freeze several hours or overnight till firm.

In mixer bowl prepare meringue by beating egg whites, vanilla, and cream of tartar till soft peaks form. Gradually add sugar, beating to stiff peaks. Combine mincemeat and sherry. Working quickly, spread mincemeat mixture over ice cream layer in pastry shell. Spread meringue over pie, carefully sealing to edge of pastry. Swirl meringue to make peaks. Place pie plate on baking sheet. Bake in 475° oven for 3 to 5 minutes or till golden. Slice pie and serve immediately.

Strawberry Sunshine Pie

**Pastry for Single-Crust Pie
 (see recipe, page 84)**
1 **pint lemon or orange sherbet**
2 **cups fresh strawberries, sliced**
1 **tablespoon sugar**
3 **egg whites**
½ **teaspoon vanilla**
¼ **teaspoon cream of tartar**
⅓ **cup sugar**

Prepare and roll out pastry. Line a 9-inch pie plate. Trim to ½ inch beyond edge of pie plate. Flute edge; prick pastry. Bake in 450° oven for 10 to 12 minutes or till golden. Cool thoroughly on wire rack.

In mixing bowl soften sherbet using a wooden spoon to stir and press against side of bowl. Soften till just pliable. Using a metal spatula, spread sherbet in baked pastry shell. Freeze several hours or overnight till firm.

Combine strawberries and 1 tablespoon sugar; set aside. In mixer bowl prepare meringue by beating egg whites, vanilla, and cream of tartar till soft peaks form. Gradually add ⅓ cup sugar, beating to stiff peaks. Working quickly, arrange strawberry-sugar mixture over sherbet layer in pastry shell. Spread meringue over berries, carefully sealing to edge of pastry. Bake on baking sheet in 475° oven for 3 to 5 minutes or till golden. Slice pie and serve immediately.

Orange-Mincemeat Tarts

**Pastry for Single-Crust Pie
 (see recipe, page 84)**
1 **quart vanilla ice cream**
1 **cup prepared mincemeat**
1 **teaspoon finely shredded
 orange peel**
Unsweetened whipped cream
**Slivered toasted almonds or
 finely shredded orange peel**

Prepare and roll out pastry to a 13-inch circle. Cut circle into six 4½-inch rounds. Place each circle over bottom of a 6-ounce custard cup. Make pleats so pastry will fit closely to cups. Prick pastry with tines of a fork. Place cups on baking sheet. Bake in 475° oven for 8 to 10 minutes or till golden. Cool thoroughly on wire rack.

In mixing bowl soften ice cream using a wooden spoon to stir and press against side of bowl. Soften till just pliable. Fold in mincemeat and 1 teaspoon orange peel. Spoon ice cream-mincemeat mixture into baked tart shells. Freeze several hours or overnight till firm.

Before serving, top each filled tart with unsweetened whipped cream. Sprinkle with some toasted almonds or additional shredded orange peel. Makes 6 tarts.

Coffee Angel Pie

Meringue Crust
   (see recipe, page 92)
1 pint coffee ice cream
1 pint vanilla ice cream
½ cup packed brown sugar
1 tablespoon cornstarch
¼ teaspoon salt
¼ cup water
⅓ cup light cream
2 tablespoons light corn syrup
¼ cup coarsely chopped pecans
1 tablespoon butter *or* margarine
1 tablespoon rum *or* brandy

Prepare Meringue Crust. Spread mixture in a well-buttered 9-inch pie plate, building up sides to form a shell. Bake in 275° oven for 1 hour. Turn off heat; let dry in oven (with door closed) for 1 hour more. Cool. Arrange scoops of coffee and vanilla ice cream in baked meringue shell. Freeze several hours or overnight till firm.

About 1 hour before serving, prepare caramel sauce. In heavy saucepan combine brown sugar, cornstarch, and salt. Stir in water. Stir in light cream and corn syrup. Cook, stirring constantly, till thickened and bubbly (mixture may appear curdled during cooking). Stir in coarsely chopped pecans, butter or margarine, and rum or brandy. Remove from heat; cover. Cool to room temperature.

Let pie stand about 10 minutes at room temperature before serving. Drizzle some of the caramel sauce over coffee and vanilla ice cream scoops. Slice pie and serve immediately with the remaining caramel sauce.

Grasshopper Pie

Chocolate Wafer Crust
   (see recipe, page 92)
6½ cups tiny marshmallows (about
   11½ ounces)
¼ cup milk
¼ cup green crème de menthe
2 tablespoons white
   crème de cacao
2 cups whipping cream
Unsweetened whipped cream
Chocolate curls

Prepare Chocolate Wafer Crust. Press crumb mixture onto bottom and sides of a 9-inch pie plate. Chill till firm.

For filling, in large saucepan combine marshmallows and milk. Cook over low heat, stirring constantly, till marshmallows are melted. Remove from heat. Cool mixture, stirring every 5 minutes. Combine crème de menthe and crème de cacao; stir into marshmallow mixture. Whip 2 cups whipping cream till soft peaks form. Fold marshmallow mixture into the whipped cream; turn into chilled wafer crust. Freeze several hours or overnight till firm. Before serving, garnish pie with additional unsweetened whipped cream and chocolate curls.

Peanut-Ice Cream Pie (pictured on page 4)

1½ cups granola
1 tablespoon butter *or* margarine,
   melted
1 quart vanilla ice cream
½ cup chunk-style peanut butter
½ of a 4½-ounce container (1 cup)
   frozen whipped dessert
   topping, thawed
2 tablespoons fudge topping
Chopped peanuts

Break up any large chunks of granola. In mixing bowl combine granola and melted butter or margarine; mix till cereal is well-coated. Press granola mixture onto bottom and sides of a well-buttered 9-inch pie plate. Bake in 375° oven for 5 to 6 minutes. Cool thoroughly on wire rack.

In mixing bowl soften ice cream using wooden spoon to stir and press against side of bowl. Soften till just pliable. Working quickly, fold in peanut butter, then whipped dessert topping. Turn ice cream mixture into granola crust. Drizzle with fudge topping. (If topping is too thick, thin with a little water.) Freeze pie several hours or overnight till firm.

Let pie stand about 10 minutes at room temperature before serving. Sprinkle with chopped peanuts. Slice pie and serve immediately.

Instead of "pie a la mode," try a switch with these cool and delicious ice-cream-filled pies. Enjoy *Coffee Angel Pie* drizzled with caramel-pecan sauce, or frosty *Grasshopper Pie*.

Banana Split Pie

**Pastry for Single-Crust Pie
(see recipe, page 84)**
2   **medium bananas**
1   **tablespoon lemon juice**
1   **quart strawberry ice cream**
½   **of a 4½-ounce container
(1 cup) frozen whipped
dessert topping, thawed**
⅓   **cup maraschino cherries (12)**
2   **tablespoons chopped walnuts**
½   **cup tiny marshmallows**
¼   **cup semisweet chocolate pieces**
2   **tablespoons milk**

Prepare and roll out pastry. Line a 9-inch pie plate. Trim pastry to ½ inch beyond edge of pie plate. Flute edge; prick bottom and sides of pastry with tines of a fork. Bake in 450° oven for 10 to 12 minutes or till golden. Cool thoroughly on wire rack.

Thinly slice bananas and sprinkle with lemon juice. Arrange the bananas on bottom of baked pastry shell. In mixing bowl soften strawberry ice cream using a wooden spoon to stir and press against side of bowl. Soften till just pliable. Using a metal spatula, spread the softened strawberry ice cream over the sliced bananas in pastry shell. Freeze till ice cream is firm.

Spread the whipped dessert topping over the frozen ice cream layer in the baked pastry shell. Top with the whole maraschino cherries; sprinkle with the chopped walnuts. Return the pie to freezer; freeze several hours or till firm.

Meanwhile, to prepare fudge sauce, in saucepan combine marshmallows, semisweet chocolate pieces, and milk. Cook over low heat, stirring constantly, till marshmallows and chocolate pieces are melted and thoroughly combined.

Let pie stand about 30 minutes at room temperature before serving. Drizzle warm or cool fudge sauce over pie. Slice pie and serve immediately.

Peach-Sauced Ice Cream Pie

**Pastry for Single-Crust Pie
(see recipe, page 84)**
1   **16-ounce can peach slices**
½   **cup crumbled soft coconut
macaroons (3 cookies)**
2   **tablespoons orange liqueur**
1   **quart vanilla ice cream**
½   **cup whipping cream**
1   **tablespoon sugar**
2   **teaspoons cornstarch**
2   **tablespoons orange liqueur**

Prepare and roll out pastry. Line a 9-inch pie plate. Trim pastry to ½ inch beyond edge of pie plate. Flute edge; prick pastry with tines of a fork. Bake in 450° oven for 10 to 12 minutes or till golden. Cool thoroughly on wire rack.

Drain peaches, reserving syrup. Finely chop *half* of the peaches. Cut the remaining peaches into chunks and set aside. Soak the crumbled coconut macaroons in 2 tablespoons orange liqueur.

In mixing bowl soften vanilla ice cream using a wooden spoon to stir and press against side of bowl. Soften till just pliable. Stir in the soaked crumbled macaroons and finely chopped peaches. Whip cream till soft peaks form. Fold whipped cream into ice cream-macaroon mixture. Turn into baked pastry shell. Freeze several hours or overnight till firm.

Just before serving, prepare peach sauce. In saucepan combine sugar and cornstarch. Stir in the remaining 2 tablespoons orange liqueur and the reserved peach syrup. Cook, stirring constantly, till thickened and bubbly. Stir in the reserved peach chunks.

Let pie stand about 10 minutes at room temperature before serving. Slice pie and drizzle the warm peach sauce over individual servings.

Neapolitan Ice Cream Pie

Coconut Crust
  (see recipe, page 93)
1 pint vanilla ice cream
1 cup dairy sour cream
3 tablespoons light rum
1 pint chocolate ice cream
1 pint strawberry ice cream
½ square (½ ounce) semisweet
  chocolate
1 teaspoon butter *or* margarine

Prepare Coconut Crust. Press coconut mixture onto bottom and sides of a buttered 9-inch pie plate. Bake in 325° oven about 20 minutes or till golden. Chill.

In mixing bowl soften vanilla ice cream using a wooden spoon to stir and press against side of bowl. Soften till just pliable. Combine sour cream and light rum; stir into softened vanilla ice cream. Freeze ice cream mixture till nearly firm. Using metal spatula, spread the vanilla ice cream mixture into baked crust. Arrange scoops of chocolate and strawberry ice cream over vanilla ice cream layer. Freeze several hours or overnight till firm.

Before serving, in small saucepan combine semisweet chocolate and butter or margarine; heat over low heat till melted, stirring constantly. Remove pie from the freezer. Drizzle the warm chocolate mixture over ice cream pie. Slice pie and serve immediately.

Frosty Pineapple Pie

Pecan Pastry
  (see recipe, page 90)
1 8¼-ounce can crushed
  pineapple
1 egg white
½ cup sugar
1 tablespoon lemon juice
1½ cups whipping cream
⅔ cup flaked coconut
Pecan halves

Prepare and roll out Pecan Pastry. Line a 9-inch pie plate. Trim to ½ inch beyond edge of pie plate. Flute edge; prick pastry. Bake in 450° oven for 10 to 12 minutes or till golden. Cool thoroughly on wire rack.

Drain pineapple, reserving ¼ cup of the syrup. In mixer bowl beat egg white till soft peaks form. Gradually add ¼ cup of the sugar, beating to stiff peaks. Gradually beat in the reserved ¼ cup pineapple syrup and the lemon juice. Whip cream and remaining ¼ cup sugar till soft peaks form. Fold coconut, drained pineapple, and egg white mixture into whipped cream. Turn fruit-cream mixture into baked pastry shell. Freeze several hours or overnight till firm. Let pie stand about 20 minutes at room temperature before serving. Garnish with pecan halves. Slice pie and serve immediately.

Cranberry-Cheese Pie

Vanilla Wafer Crust
  (see recipe, page 92)
1 14-ounce can *sweetened
  condensed* milk
⅓ cup lemon juice
½ teaspoon vanilla
2 3-ounce packages cream
  cheese, cut into cubes and
  softened
1 16-ounce can whole cranberry
  sauce
Unsweetened whipped cream

Prepare Vanilla Wafer Crust. Press crumb mixture onto bottom and sides of a 9-inch pie plate. Chill till firm. In blender container combine sweetened condensed milk, lemon juice, and vanilla; add softened cream cheese. Cover and blend till mixture is smooth. Set aside a few whole cranberries from canned sauce for garnish. Fold remaining cranberry sauce into cream cheese mixture. Pour cranberry-cream cheese mixture into chilled wafer crust. Freeze pie several hours or overnight till firm.

Let pie stand about 10 minutes at room temperature before serving. Garnish with unsweetened whipped cream and reserved whole cranberries. Slice pie and serve immediately.

Sherried Grape Chantilly Pie

Vanilla Wafer Crust
   (see recipe, page 92)
⅓ cup cream sherry
 1 package fluffy white frosting mix
   (for 2-layer cake)
 1 cup small curd cream-style
   cottage cheese
 1 cup dairy sour cream
¼ cup grape jelly
 1 tablespoon cream sherry
 1 cup red grapes, halved, seeded,
   and drained

Prepare Vanilla Wafer Crust. Press onto bottom and sides of a 9-inch pie plate. Chill. Add enough water to the ⅓ cup sherry to measure ½ cup liquid. In saucepan heat the ½ cup liquid till boiling. Pour hot liquid over frosting mix in mixer bowl; beat 7 minutes at high speed of electric mixer. Place cottage cheese and sour cream in blender container. Cover and blend till smooth. Pour mixture into a bowl; fold in frosting mixture. Turn cottage cheese-frosting mixture into wafer crust. Freeze pie several hours or overnight till firm.

Shortly before serving, combine grape jelly and the 1 tablespoon sherry in small saucepan. Cook and stir till boiling; boil 1 minute more. Remove from heat; cool to lukewarm. Just before serving, remove pie from freezer. Arrange grape halves on top of pie. Glaze grapes with jelly mixture. Slice pie and serve immediately.

Mocha Marshmallow Pie

Pastry for Single-Crust Pie
   (see recipe, page 84)
 1 6-ounce package (1 cup)
   semisweet chocolate pieces
¼ cup water
 1 tablespoon instant coffee
   crystals
 2 slightly beaten egg yolks
 1 7-, 9-, or 10-ounce jar
   marshmallow creme
 1 teaspoon vanilla
   Few drops almond extract
 2 stiff-beaten egg whites
 1 cup whipping cream
   Unsweetened whipped cream
   (optional)
 2 tablespoons crushed
   peppermint candy (optional)

Prepare and roll out pastry. Line a 9-inch pie plate. Trim to ½ inch beyond edge. Flute edge; prick pastry. Bake in 450° oven for 10 to 12 minutes or till golden. Cool thoroughly on wire rack.

In saucepan combine chocolate pieces, water, coffee crystals, and dash *salt*. Cook over low heat just till chocolate is melted, stirring frequently. Stir about *half* the hot mixture into egg yolks; return to remaining hot mixture in saucepan. Cook and stir over medium heat for 3 minutes; remove from heat. Stir in marshmallow creme, vanilla, and almond extract. Pour into large mixing bowl; cover and chill about 30 minutes. Fold in beaten egg whites. Whip 1 cup whipping cream till soft peaks form; fold into egg white mixture. Turn into pastry shell. Freeze several hours or overnight till firm.

Garnish pie with additional unsweetened whipped cream and crushed peppermint candy, if desired. Let stand about 10 minutes at room temperature before serving. Slice pie and serve immediately.

Nesselrode Pie

Vanilla Wafer Crust
   (see recipe, page 92)
 3 egg whites
¼ cup granulated sugar
¾ cup coarsely chopped
   toasted almonds
⅓ cup maraschino cherries,
   quartered
 2 tablespoons maraschino
   cherry syrup
 1 teaspoon vanilla
1½ cups whipping cream
⅓ cup sifted powdered sugar

Prepare Vanilla Wafer Crust. Press onto bottom and sides of a 9-inch pie plate. Chill. In mixer bowl beat egg whites till soft peaks form. Gradually add granulated sugar, beating to stiff peaks. Fold in almonds, quartered maraschino cherries, cherry syrup, and vanilla. Whip cream and powdered sugar till soft peaks form; fold into egg white-cherry mixture. Turn into wafer crust. Freeze several hours or overnight till firm. Let stand at room temperature 15 minutes before serving. Garnish with additional maraschino cherries, if desired.

6 Pie Crusts and Toppers

Making tender, flaky pastry from scratch is deliciously rewarding. You'll find that with a little practice and the helpful how-to steps in this section, you'll make perfect pastry and meringue every time.

Hawaiian Apple Pie
(see recipe, page 13)

Create a Pie Crust

Pastry for Single-Crust Pie

1¼ **cups all-purpose flour**
½ **teaspoon salt**
⅓ **cup shortening *or* lard**
3 **to 4 tablespoons cold water**

1 In medium mixing bowl stir together flour and salt. Cut in shortening or lard till pieces are the size of small peas. **2** Sprinkle *1 tablespoon* of the water over part of the mixture; gently toss with a fork. Push to side of bowl. Repeat till all is moistened. **3** Form dough into a ball.

4 On lightly floured surface flatten dough with hands. Roll dough from center to edge, forming a circle about 12 inches in diameter. **5** Wrap pastry around rolling pin. **6** Unroll onto a 9-inch pie plate. **7** Ease pastry into pie plate, being careful to avoid stretching pastry. **8** Trim pastry to ½ inch beyond edge of pie plate. **9-11** Make a fluted, rope-shaped, or scalloped edge.

12 For a baked pie shell, prick bottom and sides with tines of a fork. Bake in 450° oven for 10 to 12 minutes. **13** *Or,* line pastry with foil and fill with dry beans (pictured on page 83) or line the pastry with double thickness heavy-duty foil. Bake in 450° oven for 5 minutes. Remove beans and foil or heavy-duty foil; bake for 5 to 7 minutes more or till golden. Makes one 9-inch pastry shell.

Note: When you use commercial frozen pie crusts, remember that one of our pie filling recipes will fill two regular frozen pie crusts or one deep-dish frozen pie crust.

1
Stir together the flour and the salt. Cut in shortening or lard till pieces are the size of small peas, as shown.

Use a pastry blender or blending fork for cutting in shortening or lard. Mixing by hand tends to soften the shortening, making a sticky, hard-to-handle dough.

2
Sprinkle 1 tablespoon water over part of mixture; gently toss with a fork. Push to side of bowl. Repeat with the remaining water till all the flour mixture is moistened. The dough should be stiff, but not crumbly. If too much water is used, the pastry will be tough and may shrink; if too little is used, it will be crumbly.

3
Once all the flour mixture is moistened, form dough into a ball with a fork. Do not over-mix or the dough will become tough.

For a double-crust pie or a lattice-top pie (see recipe on page 87), divide the prepared dough into 2 equal parts and form into 2 rounded balls.

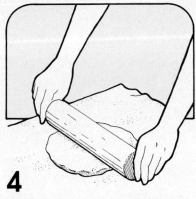

4

Turn pastry onto lightly floured surface (a pastry cloth is ideal to prevent sticking). Flatten dough and smooth edges with hands.

Roll dough from center to edge with light, even strokes, forming a circle about 12 inches in diameter (about ⅛ inch thick). Reshape into a circle with your hands as you work.

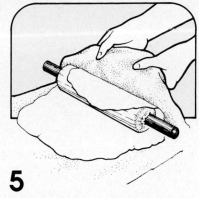

5

Use a floured rolling pin or one with a floured cover, as shown. Add only as little flour as needed, or pastry may become tough. For easy transfer to the pie plate, wrap pastry around rolling pin. To do this, gently lift pastry with hands. Or, lift pastry cloth so that pastry slides onto rolling pin and rolls around the pin, as shown.

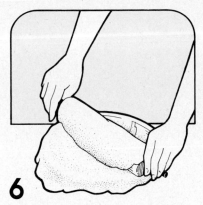

6

Loosely unroll pastry onto a 9-inch pie plate. To repair tears, moisten edges with some water and press together.

Use glass, ceramic, or dull metal pans for baking pies and pie shells. These absorb heat to brown the crust. Shiny metal pans should not be used; they reflect heat and may produce a soggy crust.

7

Ease the rolled pastry onto the pie plate. Be especially careful to avoid stretching the pastry. If the pastry is stretched, it will shrink when baked.

There should be excess pastry over the pie plate rim. Do not force this excess into the pie plate as it will produce a thicker, tougher pie crust.

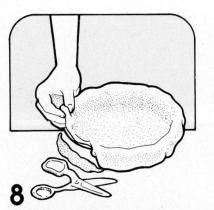

8

Use kitchen shears or a sharp knife to carefully trim the pastry to ½ inch beyond the edge of the pie plate. Fold under the extra ½ inch of pastry to build up the edge, as shown. This extra thickness of pastry will form the ridge for fluting.

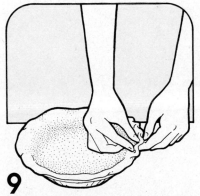

9

For a fluted edge, press dough with the forefinger (from outside the pie plate) against the thumb and forefinger of the other hand (placed inside the pie plate), as shown. Continue till entire edge is fluted. Press fluted edge against rim of pie plate. For other ways to flute pastry, see page 86.

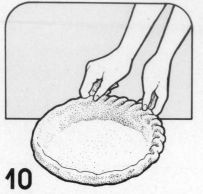

10

To create a rope-shaped edge, press dough between thumb and bent finger. While pressing, push slightly forward on slant with finger and pull back with thumb. Place thumb in dent left by finger; repeat around the edge of pie plate.

11

To create a scalloped edge, use a round-bowled measuring tablespoon to press against thumb and index finger of other hand.

12

If pastry is to be baked without a filling, prick bottom and sides of pastry all over with a fork. This helps prevent the crust from puffing up by allowing steam to escape. *(Do not prick pastry if filling is baked along with the crust.)* Bake the pricked pastry in 450° oven for 10 to 12 minutes or till it is golden. Cool on rack.

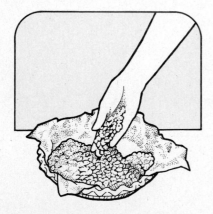

13

For a more uniformly shaped pastry shell, after pricking the shell with a fork line it with foil and fill with dry beans to prevent the crust from puffing. (Or, line pastry shell with a double thickness of heavy-duty foil; press down firmly but carefully.) The weight of the beans or foil keeps the pastry in shape. Bake pastry in 450° oven for 5 minutes. Remove beans and foil, continue baking 5 to 7 minutes more or till pastry is golden.

If a recipe calls for partially baking an *unpricked* pastry before adding the filling (such as for custard pies), use only this method of filling the pastry shell with foil and/or beans to keep the pastry in shape. Partially bake pastry in 450° oven for 5 minutes.

Pie-Making Tips

- The "secret" of pastry making is measuring accurately.
- To measure flour, stir it in the canister to lighten it. Then gently spoon it into a dry measure and level off the top with a metal spatula. (Too much flour makes the pastry tough.)
- To measure solid shortening, pack it into a dry measure. Run spatula through shortening in cup to make sure there are no air pockets remaining. (Too much shortening makes pastry greasy and crumbly.)
- To measure water for pastry, fill a measuring tablespoon to the top. Sprinkle 1 tablespoon water at a time over the flour-shortening mixture. (Too much water makes pastry soggy.)

Pastry for Double-Crust Pie

2 **cups all-purpose flour**
1 **teaspoon salt**
⅔ **cup shortening *or* lard**
6 **to 7 tablespoons cold water**
   Desired pie filling
   Milk and sugar (optional)

In medium mixing bowl stir together flour and salt. Cut in shortening or lard till pieces are the size of small peas. Sprinkle *1 tablespoon* water over part of mixture; gently toss with a fork. Push to side of bowl. Repeat till all is moistened. Form dough into 2 balls. (See steps 1-3 on page 84.)

1 On lightly floured surface flatten 1 ball of dough with hands. Roll dough from center to edge, forming a circle about 12 inches in diameter. Ease pastry into pie plate, being careful to avoid stretching pastry. Trim pastry even with rim of pie plate. **2** For top crust, roll out second ball of dough. Cut slits for escape of steam. **3** Place desired pie filling in pie shell. Top with pastry for top crust. Trim top crust ½ inch beyond edge of pie plate. **4** Fold extra pastry under bottom crust; flute edge. **5** Using pastry brush, brush pastry with some milk; sprinkle with a little sugar, if desired. **6** To prevent overbrowning, cover edge of pie with foil. Bake as directed in individual recipe. Remove foil after about half the baking time to allow crust to brown.

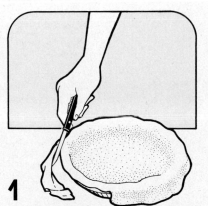

1
To make bottom crust, place 1 ball of dough on a floured surface. Flatten with hands; roll out to form circle about 12 inches in diameter. Ease pastry into pie plate, being careful to avoid stretching pastry. (See steps 4-7 on page 85.) Using a sharp knife, trim bottom crust even with rim of the pie plate.

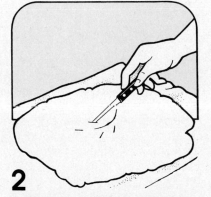

2
For top crust, roll out second ball of dough. Cut slits in top crust in a decorative design. The slits allow steam to escape while the pie is baking, keeping the underside of the crust from becoming soggy and preventing steam pressure from tearing the crust.

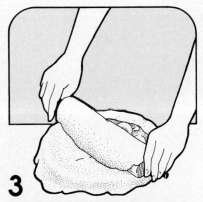

3
Place the desired pie filling in the prepared pie shell. Referring to steps 5 and 6 on page 85, gently wrap the pastry around the rolling pin and slowly unroll onto the filled pie, being careful not to stretch the pastry. If the pastry is stretched, it will shrink when baked.

4

Use kitchen shears or a sharp knife to trim the edge of the top pastry to ½ inch beyond the edge of the pie plate. Fold the extra pastry under the edge of the bottom crust to build up the edge, as shown.

Flute pie as directed in steps 9-11 on pages 85 and 86.

5

To obtain a browner, glazed-looking top crust or lattice top, use a pastry brush to brush pastry with a little milk. Lightly sprinkle pastry with some granulated sugar before baking pie.

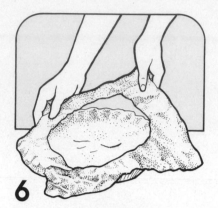

6

To prevent overbrowning, cover edge of pie with foil. Fold a 12-inch square of foil into quarters; cut an 8-inch circle from center. Unfold; place over pie, molding over edge. *Or,* cut long, narrow strips of foil to mold around edge. Bake according to individual recipe. Remove foil after about half the baking time to allow edge to brown.

Pie-Making Tips

• Simplify your pie making with the following equipment: a pastry blender to cut in shortening, a rolling pin with a stockinette cover and a pastry cloth (to prevent pastry from sticking), and a pastry wheel to cut pastry strips.

• To use a pastry cloth, sprinkle it with some flour, then rub it in. As you work, you may need to add a little more, but don't use extra flour unless the dough is sticking, or pastry can become tough. After use, the pastry cloth may be washed with your laundry. Or, if it doesn't appear fat-soaked, store it in the refrigerator. (This will prevent any fat that did adhere from becoming rancid.)

• Use a glass pie plate or a dull metal pie plate for making pies. The shiny metal pans keep the crust from browning properly.

• Cool baked pies on a wire rack set on the counter. The rack allows air to circulate under the pie, preventing it from becoming soggy from the steam remaining in it.

• When making pies at high altitudes, pie crusts are not greatly affected. A slight increase in liquid may help keep them from becoming dry. But use as little flour as possible when rolling out the dough.

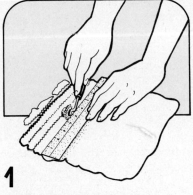

1

Lattice-Top Pie: Prepare Pastry for Double-Crust Pie (see recipe, page 87).

Roll out dough for bottom crust and line pie plate as described in steps 4-7 on page 85. Trim bottom crust to ½ inch beyond edge of pie plate.

Roll out second ball of dough. Cut dough into ½- to ¾-inch strips with a pastry wheel or sharp knife. Use a ruler to keep strips straight.

2

Place the desired fruit pie filling in the bottom pastry shell. Carefully lay half of the cut strips atop the filled pie, spacing strips at 1-inch intervals and all in the same direction, as shown.

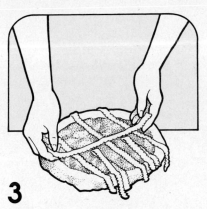

3

Carefully fold back alternate strips already in place atop fruit filling. Place another cut pastry strip in center of pie at right angles to the pastry strips that are already in place, as shown.

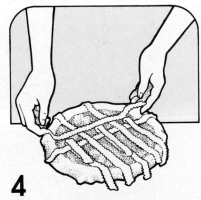

4

Slowly unfold the folded pastry strips and fold back the strips that were straight. Add another pastry strip at right angles to the folded strips and 1 inch away from the last strip, as shown. Repeat this weaving process till the lattice top is completed.

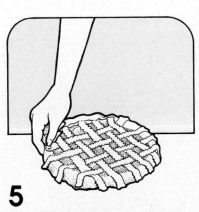

5

Trim the pastry strips even with the bottom crust. Fold bottom pastry over the lattice strips to build up the edge. Seal and flute edge, referring to steps 9-11 on pages 85 and 86.

Brush pastry with milk and sprinkle with some granulated sugar before baking, if desired. Adjust foil as described in step 6 on page 88. Bake as directed.

6

For an easy lattice, cut pastry into ½-inch strips. Lay half the strips 1 inch apart across pie (twist strips, if desired). Arrange remaining strips in diamond-shaped pattern, as shown. Press ends of strips into rim of crust. Fold bottom pastry over the lattice strips; seal and flute.

Create a Meringue Topping

Meringue for Pie

3 egg whites*
½ teaspoon vanilla
¼ teaspoon cream of tartar
6 tablespoons sugar

1 In a medium mixer bowl beat the egg whites, vanilla, and cream of tartar at medium speed of electric mixer for about 1 minute or till soft peaks form.

2-3 Gradually add the sugar, about 1 tablespoon at a time, beating at high speed of electric mixer about 4 minutes more or till mixture forms stiff, glossy peaks and sugar is dissolved.

4 Immediately spread meringue over pie, carefully sealing to edge of pastry to prevent shrinkage. Bake as directed in individual pie filling recipe.

*Note: While the 3-egg-white recipe makes an adequate amount of meringue, you can use the extra egg white from a 4-egg-yolk pie for a more generous meringue. Follow the directions above, *except* use *4* egg whites, *1 teaspoon* vanilla, *½ teaspoon* cream of tartar, and *½ cup* sugar. It may be necessary to beat the mixture slightly longer to achieve the proper consistency.

1
To make meringue, in mixer bowl beat egg whites with the vanilla and cream of tartar at medium speed of electric mixer about 1 minute or till soft peaks form.

The egg white foam will turn white and the tips of the peaks will bend over in soft curls when beaters are removed, as shown.

2
Gradually add the sugar, about a tablespoon at a time, beating at high speed of electric mixer about 4 minutes more or till mixture forms stiff, glossy peaks. Using a rubber spatula, guide egg whites toward beaters to thoroughly beat in sugar.

3

When the mixture reaches stiff peaks, the foam becomes even whiter and forms glossy peaks that stand up straight when beaters are removed, as shown.

Rub a little meringue between your fingers. If sugar is completely dissolved, you will not feel any granules.

4

Immediately spread the meringue over the hot filling. Spoon meringue around the edges first, spreading toward the center. Seal meringue to the crust all around pie to prevent shrinkage of the meringue during baking.

Bake pie as directed in individual pie filling recipe.

5

Be creative when decorating the tops of pies, tortes, or tarts.

Prepare a 3- or 4-egg-white meringue. Spoon some meringue into a pre-shaped plastic decorating bag fitted with a star tube (such as tube number 22). Pipe star or rosette designs over entire surface of pie.

Whipped cream trims:
Whipped cream works equally well in a pre-shaped plastic decorating bag fitted with a star tube. Pipe the whipped cream in a circular motion to create a shell design over surface of pie. Garnish with fruit twists, mint leaves, or chocolate curls. Try other decorating tubes for different garnishing effects.

For an easier garnishing technique using whipped cream, spoon dollops of whipped cream onto surface of pie or tarts.

You also can substitute frozen whipped dessert topping, thawed, or packaged dessert topping mix, but they will be sweeter than dairy whipping cream.

Pie-Making Tips

• It's easier to separate cold eggs, but bring them to room temperature before beating for best results. Separate eggs carefully; even the smallest amount of egg yolk can prevent the whites from whipping.

• Wash beaters thoroughly before beating egg whites. Use a deep, straight-sided glass or metal bowl; do not use a plastic bowl, since the oils retained in the plastic prevent the egg whites from forming peaks.

• For best results when whipping cream, thoroughly chill the mixer bowl and the beaters. Beat the well-chilled whipping cream to stiff peaks. Peaks should stand up when beaters are removed. Do not overbeat.

Meringue Crust

2 **egg whites**
½ **teaspoon vanilla**
¼ **teaspoon salt**
¼ **teaspoon cream of tartar**
½ **cup sugar**
½ **cup finely chopped pecans**

In mixer bowl beat together egg whites, vanilla, salt, and cream of tartar till soft peaks form. Gradually add sugar and beat to stiff peaks and till sugar is dissolved. Fold in chopped pecans. Spread mixture onto bottom and sides of a well-buttered 9-inch pie plate, building up the sides with a spoon to form a shell. Bake in 300° oven for 50 minutes. Turn off heat and let dry in oven with door closed for 2 hours more. Cool thoroughly on rack.

Graham Cracker Crust

18 **graham cracker squares**
¼ **cup sugar**
6 **tablespoons butter *or* margarine, melted**

Place graham crackers in a plastic bag or between 2 sheets of plastic wrap or waxed paper. Crush into fine crumbs; measure 1¼ cups crumbs. (Or, crush crackers into fine crumbs in blender.) Place crumbs in medium mixing bowl; stir in sugar. Stir melted butter or margarine into crumb mixture; toss to thoroughly combine.

Turn the crumb-butter mixture into a 9-inch pie plate. Spread the crumb mixture evenly in the pie plate. Press onto the bottom and sides to form a firm, even crust. Chill about 1 hour or till firm. (*Or,* bake in 375° oven for 6 to 9 minutes or till edges are brown. Cool on rack before filling.)

Gingersnap-Graham Crust

¾ **cup fine gingersnap crumbs (12 cookies)**
½ **cup fine graham cracker crumbs (7 crackers)**
¼ **cup butter *or* margarine, melted**
2 **tablespoons sugar**

In mixing bowl toss together gingersnap crumbs, graham cracker crumbs, melted butter or margarine, and sugar. Turn crumb mixture into a 9-inch pie plate. Spread the crumb mixture evenly in the pie plate. Press onto bottom and sides to form a firm, even crust. Bake in 375° oven for 4 to 5 minutes. Cool thoroughly on rack.

Vanilla Wafer Crust

1½ **cups finely crushed vanilla wafers (36 wafers)**
6 **tablespoons butter *or* margarine, melted**

In mixing bowl combine crushed vanilla wafers and the melted butter or margarine. Turn crumb mixture into a 9-inch pie plate. Spread the crumb mixture evenly in the pie plate. Press onto bottom and sides to form a firm, even crust. Chill about 1 hour or till firm.

Chocolate Wafer Crust

1½ **cups finely crushed chocolate wafers (25 wafers)**
6 **tablespoons butter *or* margarine, melted**

In mixing bowl combine crushed wafers and the melted butter or margarine. Turn the chocolate crumb mixture into a 9-inch pie plate. Spread the crumb mixture evenly in the pie plate. Press onto bottom and sides to form a firm, even crust. Chill about 1 hour or till firm.

Coconut Crust

2 cups flaked coconut
3 tablespoons butter *or* margarine, melted

In mixing bowl combine coconut and the melted butter or margarine. Turn the coconut mixture into a 9-inch pie plate. Spread the mixture evenly in the pie plate. Press onto bottom and sides to form a firm, even crust. Bake in 325° oven about 20 minutes or till coconut is golden. Cool thoroughly on rack.

Pecan Pastry

Pastry for Single-Crust Pie (see recipe, page 84)
3 tablespoons finely chopped pecans

Prepare single-crust pastry *except* add the chopped pecans before adding water. Roll out and bake pastry as directed.

If individual recipe calls a double-crust pecan pastry, prepare pastry for Double-Crust Pie (see recipe, page 87) *except* add ⅓ cup finely chopped pecans before adding water. Roll out and bake pastry as directed.

Oil Pastry

2¼ cups all-purpose flour
1 teaspoon salt
¼ cup cooking oil
6 tablespoons cold milk

In mixing bowl stir together flour and salt. Pour cooking oil and milk into measuring cup (do not stir); add all at once to flour mixture. Stir lightly with a fork. Form into 2 balls; flatten slightly with hands.

Cut waxed paper into four 12-inch squares. Place each ball of dough between 2 squares of paper. Roll each ball of dough into circle to edges of paper. (Dampen tabletop with a little water to prevent paper from slipping.) Peel off top paper and fit dough, paper side up, into pie plate. Remove paper. Finish as for a basic single- or double-crust pastry (see pages 84 to 88). Makes two 9-inch single-crust pastries, or one 9-inch double-crust pastry.

Electric Mixer Pastry

1¾ cups all-purpose flour
¾ teaspoon salt
¾ cup shortening
⅓ cup cold water

In small mixer bowl combine flour and salt; add shortening. Beat at low speed with electric mixer till pieces are the size of small peas. Add water; beat at low speed just till a dough begins to form (about 15 to 20 seconds). Form dough into a ball with hands. Divide into 2 balls. Roll out and finish as for a single- or double-crust pastry (see pages 84 to 88). Makes two 9-inch single-crust pastries or one 9-inch double-crust pastry.

This pastry is very easy to work with, and even rolls out easily right from the refrigerator. To make four 9-inch single-crust pastries or two 9-inch double-crust pastries, follow the above method, using a large mixer bowl, *except* use 3¾ *cups* all-purpose flour, *1½* teaspoons salt, *1½ cups* shortening, and ¾ *cup* cold water. Shape dough into 4 balls. Wrap in clear plastic wrap; store in refrigerator up to 2 weeks.

Index